THE
MEDICAL
PRACTICE
Start-Up
GUIDE

THE MEDICAL PRACTICE *Start-Up* GUIDE

Editors

MARC D. HALLEY, MBA

MICHAEL J. FERRY, MPA

GREENBRANCH
PUBLISHING

Published by Greenbranch Publishing, LLC
PO Box 208
Phoenix, MD 21131
Phone: (800) 933-3711
Fax: (410) 329-1510
Email: info@greenbranch.com
Websites: www.mpmnetwork.com, www.mbmbuyersguide.com, www.soundpractice.net

This publication is designed to provide general medical practice management information and is sold with the understanding that neither the author nor the publisher is engaged in rendering legal, accounting, ethical, or clinical advice. If legal, technological, or other expert advice is required, the services of a competent professional person should be sought.

Printed in the United States of America by United Book Press, Inc. www.unitedbookpress.com

Publisher
Nancy Collins

Editorial Assistant
Jennifer Weiss

Production Services:
Hearthside Publishing Services

Design and Composition:
Candice Carta-Myers

Indexer:
Robert Swanson

Copyeditor:
Wesley Morrison

Marc D. Halley, MBA, is the founder of The Halley Consulting Group, LLC and has served as its CEO since 1995. The company is the culmination of many years of providing practice management and consulting to varying medical specialties, including hospital-owned primary care networks. His career in health care spans more than twenty years, and his experience includes the development of numerous tools and models now used by the firm to assist their clients in improving medical practice operations. Marc has also worked hands-on in physician recruitment, compensation, medical staff development planning, strategy and governance, contract negotiations, and medical practice network financial turnarounds.

Marc is a frequently requested speaker on physician/hospital integration issues and has authored several articles that have been published in industry magazines. In 2007, Marc "wrote the book" on hospital ownership of medical practices as a competitive strategy. *The Primary-Care Market Share Connection: How Hospitals Achieve Competitive Advantage* was published by Health Administration Press. In addition, members of Halley Consulting, including Marc, recently contributed several chapters to volume one of a three-volume set of books, *The Business of Health Care*.

Michael J. Ferry, MPA, is Vice President of Operations for The Halley Consulting Group, LLC. Michael has worked in the health care industry for more than twenty-five years in varying leadership roles for both hospitals and physician networks. He has been engaged in physician practice development for ten of these years, both working with Halley Consulting and serving as the lead operational executive for a large regional physician network affiliated with a national health care organization. Michael has specialized in both medium and large clients in his work with Halley Consulting, including networks of up to 180 physicians. He is also actively involved in providing extensive consulting services to smaller practices. This work has included practice acquisition, network start-ups and a full range of consulting and implementation activity leading to practice and network growth and improvement. Governance formation and development is a particular area of interest, and he has worked in that arena for many Halley clients.

The Halley Consulting Group works to improve the strategic and operational performance of medical practice networks nationwide. The firm's client list runs the gamut from small, independent medical offices to large, multispecialty practice networks owned and run by hospitals in some of the most competitive markets in the country. Halley Consulting

Group executives are trained and experienced implementers who have worked as leaders on the hospital side as well as in hospital-owned physician practices. Most of the firm's executives have been in the business of practice start-up and management for ten years or more. For consulting clients, the Halley Consulting deliverables define the firm as *a leading national expert in hospital-owned medical practice network management.* Their processes are always collaborative in nature, seeking to unite hospital executives and employed/affiliated physicians around shared operational objectives, policies, and processes. Their work always takes into account each client's unique operational situation. Halley Consulting's final deliverables are not cookie-cutter PowerPoint presentations; rather, they are real "playbooks" that have solid strategic and operational impact.

LIST OF CONTRIBUTORS

Andrew J. Halley, MBA, CMPE
Practice Consultant
The Halley Consulting Group, LLC
Westerville, Ohio

Marc D. Halley, MBA
President and CEO
The Halley Consulting Group, LLC
Westerville, Ohio

Michael J. Ferry, MPA
Vice President of Operations
The Halley Consulting Group, LLC
Westerville, Ohio

Brian K. Morton, MBA
Region Executive
The Halley Consulting Group, LLC
Westerville, Ohio

Michelle A. Wier, CMPE
Chief Executive Officer
Valley Medical Center
Lewiston, Idaho

CONTENTS

PREFACE

WHY?

With so many physicians exiting their training programs and looking for employment opportunities rather than entrepreneurial ventures, why write a book on starting up a medical practice? It's a fair question. The answer includes multiple components. First, you will be starting *your* medical practice even if you join a group as an employee (unless you are taking over a full practice from a retiring physician). Chapters One, Two, Four, Six, Seven, and Nine contain valuable information for *your* practice and, potentially, for your more established associates. Second, if you are planning an entrepreneurial venture, be it a brand new practice or a new group, the principles identified herein can help to ensure the success of your undertaking. They represent the best practices to date, gathered through numerous consulting and management experiences. Third, if you are a new medical practice manager, this book will provide you with the basic principles and many best practices used by more experienced managers. Finally, the accompanying tools will be of benefit to anyone involved in starting, building, or maintaining a medical practice.

The book is written for physicians, who finish their residency programs with wonderful clinical skills but without much, if any, training in medical practice management. As we note right up front, regardless of your specialty or circumstances (e.g., employee, partner, or entrepreneur), every practicing physician is "in business." Even if your interest in the business side of medicine is limited, learning a few rules or best practices in the short term might just save you significant headaches and a lot of money in the long term.

OUR QUALIFICATIONS

The Medical Practice Start-Up Guide was written by several well-experienced consultants and hands-on managers who are part of The Halley Consulting Group, LLC. Our team has more than 100 years of combined practice management and practice consulting experience. We have managed independent physician-owned practices and hospital-owned practices. We have managed numerous primary care practices, many internal medicine subspecialty groups, and several surgical practice specialties. We have managed rural practices, busy suburban group practices, inner city practices, and large, hospital-owned networks with 40 or more locations. We have recruited numerous new physicians in several specialties on behalf of our clients and started up several new practices as well as new hospital-owned medical practice networks. We have formed or merged several small group practices and even helped a few groups to separate. We have evaluated numerous individual practices, large medical networks, several billing offices, and many physician compensation models.

We are, first and foremost, managers or implementers, which we believe makes us better consultants. We have managed and consulted with new start-ups and provided interim management to established groups and networks. Importantly, we have participated in helping turn around the performance of several practices and networks that had ignored correct operating principles.

Our contributing authors are well trained-many with master's degrees. More importantly, they are all well experienced in practice management and many specific areas of interest. These content experts have lent a hand to the development and editing of various chapters, thus sharing their expertise. We acknowledge the efforts of Michelle Wier, CMPE, whose experience and research yielded a great deal of the initial text.

THE FORMAT

We have taken a risk by including specific website addresses and referencing regulations that will likely change over time. In fact, between the original writing and subsequent editing of this book, some material had to be updated as a result of recent changes. Nevertheless, we felt that our specific references would be more valuable to readers. Of course, the correct principles we have included in each of the chapters have stood the test of time and will remain valuable regardless of changes in the legal/regulatory environment or on the Internet. Finally, several chapters reference tools that are available to supplement the principles in this book. These tools are updated, as needed, to remain viable for our clients and can be accessed through the Halley Consulting website (http://www.halleyconsulting.com).

SUMMARY

Starting a medical practice properly requires tremendous time, energy, and personal commitment on the part of physicians, managers, and others. We believe that *The Medical Practice Start-Up Guide* will be a valuable tool in the development of your new practice. This work is by no means all-inclusive. We believe, however, that it will provide the reader with a solid understanding of medical practice development and help new physicians to avoid some common pitfalls as they enter the practice of medicine.

Best of luck on your new venture!

Marc D. Halley, MBA
Michael J. Ferry, MPA
Editors

CHAPTER One

THE PRACTICE CHOICE

WHAT DO I WANT TO DO?

You have spent years in school, followed by years in residency, all focused on becoming an expert in your selected clinical specialty. If you are like most new physicians, you probably have debt associated with your training. You probably have had only limited exposure to managing a medical practice. You are faced with a variety of significant decisions and multiple options that require an understanding of issues outside your training and experience. These decisions will have implications for your enjoyment of and ability to practice medicine, for your personal income, for your family situation, and more.

As physician recruiters, we learned that physicians one to two years out of residency often make great targets for recruitment, because they are disillusioned with their first real practice experience. This disillusionment occurs for a variety of reasons:

- Some physicians, when selecting their initial practice location, focus on the immediate financial rewards of certain offers to the exclusion of other important factors, such as quality of work life and quality of family life (e.g., schools, community lifestyle, and church).

- Some physicians are frustrated over slow practice growth as a result of unrealistic expectations, specialty saturation in the selected market, inability to participate with some local payers, or unwillingness on the part of potential referring physicians to change established referral patterns.

- Other physicians report a failure on the part of a hospital or host practice to understand the implications, particularly the financial implications, of starting a new medical practice.

- A few physicians experience a poor personality match with their new physician partners, making daily work life miserable.

- Other physicians report limited or poorly designed promotional tactics.

- Some physicians even report failure to employ effective support staff and/or an effective office manager as reasons for their subsequent discouragement.

No one has a crystal ball to view the future implications of each practice option, but a few key tactics can reduce the chance of making a poor practice choice when coming out of a residency program. These tactics include:

- **The Practice Ideal:** Take time to develop and *write down* your idea of the perfect practice setting. Describe that setting in as much detail as possible. Include a description of the physical location, your partners (if any), your preferred patient profile, the services you will offer, the volume of patients you will see, the payer mix, your call coverage arrangement, and so on.

- **The Family Ideal:** Take time to consider the family implications of your medical practice. Write down your ideas of the perfect family setting, including schools, religious affiliation, hobbies, sports, home setting, shopping, and so on. Discuss these considerations with your spouse and children who are old enough to participate.

- **Upper Classmen:** Maintain contact with those who have left your residency during the previous two years. Talk to them about their real-life experience and what they would have done differently, and seek their recommendations to add to your decision process.

- **Multiple Options:** Do not swing at the first pitch. Consider multiple options even if you have a favorite alternative. Use a score sheet to help you objectively rank the options against your practice and family ideals.

- **Red Flags:** Follow your instincts. If a situation does not feel right, it probably isn't. Even if the clinical opportunity seems right or the money is great or the people are nice, make the *right decision* for the *right reasons*. Be sensitive to those recruitment settings that seem disorganized. Raise a red flag if the people with whom you interview have differing opinions about your opportunity or about the "deal." Ask for a list of recently recruited physicians (those recruited during the most recent one to three years), and select a few to call and talk with about their experience.

- **Long Term:** Focus on the long term when making a practice location decision. You will be investing valuable time in developing relationships with patients and referring physicians. The right relationships, your hard work, and the right situation will ultimately yield the type of practice and the income you desire.

PRACTICE OPTIONS

Physicians leaving training today have several alternatives available to them when starting a practice. These options fall into two broad categories, entrepreneurship (or business ownership) and employment. For our purposes, we will define entrepreneurship as private solo practice as well as a partnership in physician-owned, single-specialty or multispecialty medical groups. Entrepreneurship usually involves some level of risk and investment to develop or to buy into an established practice. Entrepreneurship also includes the need to pay attention to the business side of medical practice, with potentially heavy consequences for ignorance or mistakes. Such private practice options are still available in most communities. The second category, employment, includes employment by physician-owned groups, by hospitals, and by insurance companies or others. Employment does not involve personal financial risk and may not involve much in the way of business decision making. It may also limit your freedom to practice as you see fit. Employment options are available in most communities for both primary care and specialty physicians.

Entrepreneurship

Fifty years ago, if a physician wanted to go into private practice, "he" would select a community, perhaps obtain a bank loan, "hang out a shingle," and wait for patients to come.

During the early months of the practice, the physician would make very little personal income, but over time, by word-of-mouth referrals from satisfied patients, the practice would grow. Eventually, the physician would have a full schedule of patients and earn compensation that placed him well ahead of most others in the community.

Today, very few physicians start a practice without significant external support. Large student loans, high income expectations, downward pressure on reimbursement, increased levels of competition, and desire for a better quality of life than their professional predecessors all contribute to a climate that precludes just hanging out a shingle.

Local hospitals, as part of their medical staff development efforts, have become a major source of financial and other assistance for physicians seeking to establish their own private practice or to join established groups. Much of this assistance has come in the form of income guarantees or start-up loans, which may include loan forgiveness in exchange for helping to meet the community's need for their particular specialty. (We will discuss various financing options in Chapter Two.)

Entrepreneurship provides a physician with substantial freedom to practice as he or she sees fit. Along with that freedom, however, comes substantial market and financial risk. Every medical practice has a clinical side and a business side. Physician entrepreneurs must effectively manage both. Either intuitively or otherwise, successful physicians understand the critical nature of *managing relationships* with patients and other referral sources. They understand both *clinical quality* and *service quality* and can effectively balance the two with the *personal productivity* that will ensure their ability to meet their payroll. They have natural leadership skills that inspire their partners and their support staff. They tend to be outgoing, engaged, and involved in their communities and with their medical staffs.

Employment

Increasingly, physicians completing their training programs are opting for an employment opportunity. This preference has been common among primary care providers for several years but is increasingly prevalent among new specialists—even surgical specialists—now completing their training programs. This phenomenon appears to be a function of one or more of the following factors:

- As mentioned earlier, many physicians are completing their training programs with significant debt. This burden contributes to an aversion to taking on additional financial risk.
- Despite tremendous strides in some residency programs, most new physicians are relatively unprepared to enter into small business. Many express a desire to focus on their clinical training, skills, and interests rather than to manage human resources and financial performance.
- Many younger physicians express a desire to have a better quality of work life and personal life than their predecessors had. Many young physicians prefer the camaraderie of older, experienced peers. Others do not want to work the long hours required to see patients in the hospital, in the practice, and in other locations. Still others want paid time off and the better employee benefits offered by some employers. In addition, more women have completed their training and have entered the profession in recent years, some of whom have a desire to work part time to have more family time. Most of these desires are incompatible with private practice.

Regardless of your preferred geographic location, physicians can usually find viable employment and entrepreneurial practice alternatives in nearly every community of any size and in most rural settings as well. Some opportunities even offer the chance to start out in a protected employment setting with a subsequent transfer to private ownership. The primary decision, then, is "where."

WHERE DO I WANT TO PRACTICE?

Let's get down to the process of, and resources for, making the practice location decision. Consider the following components of this critical choice:

- **Personal Issues:** Be selfish for a few moments, and think about where you want to live and work and play. Chances are that you have not spent a lot of time during your residency training contemplating such topics. Do you have a particularly favorite part of the country? Do you prefer mountains, plains, or desert? What kind of commute do you prefer? Do you like big cities or small towns? Have you decided to serve a particular population?

    A number of sources provide comparative information about communities in the United States. Websites, magazines, newspapers, and other sources routinely publish lists ranking cities on a variety of criteria. Sperling's publishes the "Best Places to Live" on an annual basis (http://www.bestplaces.net). They also publish "The Best Small Towns" and "Healthiest Cities." CNNMoney offers its own list and sublists, from "Hottest Cities" to "Least Polluted Cities" (http://money.cnn.com/best/bplive/). If a more interactive option would be helpful, several websites offer questionnaires designed to help participants match their interests and desired lifestyle with particular locales. The website "Find Your Spot" is just one example of this interactive approach (http://www.findyourspot.com/).

- **Family Issues:** For most physicians, the decision about where to practice is not just a personal decision. Many have a spouse and family or other significant relationships that they must take into consideration. Issues relating to your family unit might include the availability of a career or education path for a spouse or adequate schools for children. Proximity to aging parents or to other extended family is often important to physicians and their spouses. Religious affiliation may be an important family matter, along with the availability of preferred neighborhoods, shopping, and cultural activities.

- **Community Issues:** Beyond family issues, practicing in an urban or suburban setting with large hospitals and medical groups is vastly different from practicing in a rural setting with limited acute care services. Obviously, some specialties are restricted to more populated areas simply because of access to an acute care workshop. Primary care specialties have more options for a rural practice setting if the population is available to support one more physician in their specialty. The availability of professional camaraderie often enters into the community decision.

    In addition to the community setting, the economic viability of the community is important to consider. The availability of jobs, particularly those that offer health insurance benefits, will have a significant impact on your practice (not to mention on the physical and emotional health of the community). You should know if legislation at the state or local level may impact (positively or negatively) the community's viability and your ability to operate the business side of a medical practice.

    Sources of information regarding local community issues include the state medical society and the local chamber of commerce, which offer information and insights for little or no cost to those interested in the communities they serve.

Closely related, and often a function of economic viability, is the growth of the community population. A diverse and growing community has a positive effect on a new medical practice, providing an opportunity to attract new patients and/or new referring physicians. Conversely, a community suffering from high unemployment and a stagnant or declining population has a negative effect on medical practice development and survival.

Current and projected population data are available through a number of sources. U.S. Census data are free and offer population projections several years into the future by state, metropolitan service area, or county (http://www.census.gov). Subscription-based services offer more detailed population projections and characteristics, such as ESRI Business Information Solutions (http://www.esri.com) and Claritas (http://www.claritas.com). In addition, analysis of population trends by city, county, and state are often featured on websites (e.g., http://www.citymayors.com, http://money.cnn.com, and http://www.forbes.com).

The relative cost of living is also an important factor in your community location decision, particularly when considering the required income to make major purchases like a home. Again, CNNMoney offers a cost of living calculator (http://cgi.money.cnn.com/tools/costofliving/costofliving.html). This information can help you to assess the adequacy of employment offers you receive and/or assist in the development of pro forma financial statements for a new practice. For example, if you prefer to spend no more than twenty-five percent of your income on a home mortgage (i.e., principle, interest, insurance, and taxes), you can quickly determine whether you can afford a community given the salary/income guarantee offered or the income potential projected for your practice.

■ **Competitive Issues:** Critical to your success in any community is a clear understanding of the competitive pressures and their impact on your specialty. *Saturation* and *exclusion* are two critical competitive risks. Competing hospitals are sometimes looking to fill the same projected specialty "gaps" in a community, resulting in a saturation of that specialty. Consequently, even good physicians in the specialty struggle to build, and sometimes to maintain, a viable practice in the market. Indicators of community need for your specialty should be readily available to you through your recruiter, but it is critical that you also have enough information from physicians "on the ground" to ensure that adequate demand for your specialty exists.

In addition to the anecdotal information you will receive through interviews with physicians in your target area, you can validate community need for your specialty by dividing the current number of physicians in your specialty by the current and, then, by the future population data that you previously gathered. Comparing the resulting ratios with physician per capita ratios provided by the U.S. Department of Health and Human Services is a good general indicator of need. Current physician numbers can be found through several websites:

■ WebMD Physician Directory (http://doctor.webmd.com)
■ American Medical Association offers its own physician finder service (http://webapps.ama-assn.org/doctorfinder/html/patient.html)

- U.S. Department of Health and Human Services "State Health Workforce Profiles" (http://bhpr.hrsa.gov/healthworkforce/reports/profiles/)

  Although you may love medicine, being on call 24/7 without adequate call coverage dramatically reduces the pleasure of medical practice. In most communities, physicians end up sharing after-hours call coverage with their "competitors"—namely, other physicians in the same specialty. If there are large numbers of physicians in your specialty (and the population to support them), you are likely to find adequate opportunities to share call coverage. If not, you might be excluded from certain call groups whose members are threatened by your arrival. Make sure that call coverage is available by visiting with one or more call groups before making your community decision.

- **Payer Issues:** Your future practice will not survive on government payers only. You will need to become credentialed and participate with other commercial payers to attract patients as a primary care physician or patient referrals from primary care providers if you are a specialist. You will want to make sure that payers serving the community are accepting new physicians as participating providers in your specialty.

- **Practice Issues:** For the many physicians who will join an established practice as a partner or an employee, there are several additional considerations about the practice itself. Some physicians leave residency to join a family member or close friends in practice. Some join those who graduated from the same residency program and have already taken the risk of establishing a medical practice. Many others must hunt down established opportunities either "on their own" or with the help of a professional recruiter. Regardless of the setting, understanding not only the clinical opportunity but also the practice operation should be a critical part of your decision process. The clinical opportunity may be wonderful, but the success of practice operations will affect your success and your income dramatically. Among several practice considerations, the following should be carefully explored before making a final decision:
  - **Decision Making:** How successfully do current physicians work together to make important decisions? How do they manage disagreements among the current partners? Will you be allowed to participate in the decision-making process? What difficult decisions have been made in the practice during recent years, and how successfully were those decisions implemented?
  - **Management:** How effective is the office/practice manager? Do the current physicians have confidence in the manager and his or her abilities? Do they support the manager to implement difficult decisions? How do the support staff members feel about the manager?
  - **Human Resources:** Do all the support staff members report to the office manager? Are wage and salary levels considered fair? Does the practice have a competitive employee benefits package, including benefits for the physicians and their families? Is the staff well-trained? Do staff members get along? How much turnover has there been among staff members during the last two years?
  - **Accounts Receivable Management:** Does the billing and reimbursement process work? What percentage of gross billings is written off as contractual allowances? What percentage of gross billings is written off as bad debt or uncollectible accounts?

■ **Financial Performance:** Are there expenses that stand out as being unusually high, such as malpractice insurance or billing costs? Are the current physicians satisfied with their level of income? Is the practice able to meet its normal operating expenses without borrowing? Do the partners save a portion of their income to purchase new equipment or respond to unexpected expenses? Do the physicians fund their retirement plans?

PLACING MY PRIVATE PRACTICE

Those who have chosen to join an established practice and location in their selected community can pass over this section. For those who are starting a new practice or entering a new practice location, however, this section will be relevant. The planning process for placement of your practice will be discussed in this section.

It is said that the first three rules for establishing a successful business are location, location, location. While you do not have to worry about locating your practice next to a convenience store on the busiest intersection in town, location is important for a variety of reasons:

■ **Access:** The more convenience and ease of access you can provide to your patients/customers, the more successful your medical practice will be. Convenience and access can be significantly influenced by your location decision. Primary care physicians in urban or suburban locations must be aware that most of the patients who frequent their practices will live within a relatively short distance of the selected practice location. (Our experience indicates that most patients select a primary care practice for the family within a 10-minute drive of their homes and children's schools.)

■ **Affiliations:** Affiliations matter, and your location will likely affect your affiliations. Your hospital affiliation will also affect your specialty affiliations, your primary care affiliations, and even the payers with whom you contract. As a specialist, your ability to affiliate with a hospital that shares an interest in your specialty (e.g., as a service line) is a significant advantage. Your hospital's affiliated primary care providers and their payer contracts will also affect your ability to attract patient referrals. As a primary care physician, affiliating with a progressive hospital and its associated specialists enhances the quality of care you can offer your patients when they require more invasive services.

■ **Building Occupancy:** The cost of your physical space is usually the third-largest element in your practice cost structure and can have a dramatic effect on your personal income. Medical office space conveniently located on a hospital campus can cost $25 or more per square foot per year. Space located off campus may cost less than $15 per square foot per year. If you require 1,500 square feet of office space, the difference may be $15,000 or more each year. The availability of modern yet affordable space will be part of your location decision, and opting for a nonhospital campus setting may be your best bet to avoid the higher rates per square foot.

As a primary care provider, you will want to locate near neighborhoods that support the characteristics of your desired patient population. You will want to use many of the same resources discussed above to hone your community analysis to an individual zip code, neighborhood, or even census tract. Driving around a potential practice location can provide valuable anecdotal information about the potential patient population to supplement your statistical data. Families living in apartments, for example, tend to have lower income levels than those living in single-family dwellings. Neighborhoods full of starter homes tend to indicate young families and children. More established neighborhoods speak volumes about the resident population in terms of income, family composition, and so on. For those desiring to treat an underserved population, sites near common bus routes should be included in your location selection options and criteria. Perhaps you speak a foreign language and can offer this additional benefit if your location is accessible to concentrations of your selected population. General internists will want to locate near growing adult populations. Pediatricians will want to locate near family settings.

Some physicians may have the additional opportunity to offer services to their own race or ethnic group. For example, some patients are more comfortable seeing physicians of their own race. In a study reported in the *Annals of Family Medicine*, it was noted that twenty-two percent of African Americans preferred to see an African-American physician.[1] For Latin Americans, this preference was even higher, with thirty-three percent preferring to see a Latin-American physician.[2] Depending on your desired patient mix, you may want to consider these study results as you determine your selected location and the access it may provide.

New physicians can also benefit from the analysis of more sophisticated retail chains regarding site selection. The presence of retailers like Walgreens, CVS, Wal-Mart, Home Depot, and others (especially newer stores) is usually an indication of a strong and/or growing population in the surrounding neighborhoods. Available space within a reasonable proximity to these retailers can be a real plus for a primary care physician seeking to capture that same population.

Locating near a retail corridor is a smart move for primary care physicians in particular. From a patient's perspective, an appointment with a doctor is often another item on a long list of "to-do's" for the day. Your patients may be running errands before and/or after their appointments with you. Positioning your practice near a major retail corridor in the area will make your site comparatively more attractive as new patients realize the convenience of your location.

Critical to the success of any practice is a *sustainable* population base. Population growth projections are available from national companies like ESRI Business Information Systems and Claritas (mentioned earlier). You'll find the most reliable and customized neighborhood information, however, through the local department of community development found in many city offices. Community development staff members can tell you about specific housing developments that are planned or underway in your selected market area. In most instances, you can find details such as the location of planned developments, the number of units, the type of units, the number of sold/unsold units, and the projected completion dates. This information is invaluable for pinpointing those areas within your community where new growth is expected, which will facilitate the growth of your practice—even if established competitors are present with whom you will share a piece of a growing pie.

It is also important to be aware of zoning ordinances as you consider potential office sites. Areas zoned for professional services or office use will usually accommodate a medical practice. If other medical offices are in the area, you might become part of a "medical corridor" for patients seeking health care services.

---

[1] Chen, Frederick M., George E. Fryer, Robert L. Phillips, Elisabeth Wilson, and Donald E. Pathman. "Patients' Beliefs About Racism, Preferences for Physician Race, and Satisfaction with Care." *Annals of Family Medicine* 3 (2005); 138-143. Retrieved July 20, 2006, from http://www.annfammed.org/cgi/content/full/3/2/138.

[2] Ibid.

A commercial realtor may be able to assist you in identifying a list of potential locations that will meet your requirements. A realtor may be able to assist you in subsequent negotiations for your selected space as well. Remember, however, that the ultimate decision regarding your "business" location must be yours. Don't succumb to high-pressure sales techniques that may spell a commission for your realtor and trouble for your practice.

The presence of competitors, including substitutes for your specialty, can be a positive or a negative factor in your location decision, depending on the intensity of competition in the area. As we discussed earlier, new physicians might find themselves in a saturated market, making it difficult to build a new practice. They may even be excluded from essential call coverage arrangements if the competition is too intense. Although you may have found a community with a need for your specialty, the issue of competitive intensity should factor into your specific location decision—particularly if you are a primary care provider, who will likely draw your patient population from a relatively small area around the practice. Understanding the physician-to-population ratio within a five-mile circumference of your potential location is an important factor in your decision. Those competing physicians whose five-mile circles intersect with yours will likely share your primary market and draw from the same neighborhoods. Ideally, there should be more than enough patients to easily support your practice and others attracting patients from your five-mile circle to allow for those patients who travel outside your area to neighboring zip codes for medical services. Again, census data are usually readily available, and local hospital websites and the local telephone listings provide information on physicians in your specialty and in competing specialties.

As you conduct your physician-to-population analysis, remember that in the mind of the patient, family medicine, internal medicine, and pediatric physicians may be substitutes for one another. Include these or other relevant specialties in your analysis as well.

CHAPTER SUMMARY

You have spent years preparing to provide high-quality clinical care. Now you are faced with a myriad of choices regarding where and how you will provide that care. You may feel unprepared to make these decisions, which will clearly affect your career satisfaction and the quality of life for you and those closest to you. It is well worth the relatively few hours it will take to think about what you want in a practice setting, to consider the impact of your decision on those closest to you, to properly explore several alternatives, to conduct a bit of simple analysis, and to make the best decision given the information you collect during the process.

CHAPTER Two

PLANNING, FINANCING, AND PROTECTING YOUR BUSINESS

YOU ARE IN BUSINESS

By design, relatively few residency programs focus significantly on practice development or management. Even fewer residents focus on the subject. Suddenly, after years of clinical training, you, like many others, find yourself in the *business* of medicine. You may not have much interest in the business side of medical practice. You may even resent its influence on your clinical priorities. Even as an employee, however, business decisions will affect your daily practice. You will need to actively influence or participate in those decisions, or others will do so for you—while perhaps ignoring factors you feel are important. Our counsel to new physicians is to get involved in the business side. Your involvement will make you a better employee or partner and, ultimately, will increase your satisfaction with the clinical practice of medicine.

In this chapter, we will explore the basics of planning how you will create and operate your medical practice, how you can finance your practice, and how you can protect yourself and your business.

BUSINESS PLANS AND STRUCTURE

For those who are entering private practice, making the decision about where to practice is only part of the planning required to help ensure the success of your new venture. Planning is critical for any business venture. It is particularly critical to the success of new businesses or those experiencing a significant change, such as adding a new partner, developing a new service, or facing a new competitor. In its simplest form, the business planning process accomplishes the following:

- It helps us identify *what* business we are in and *how* we are (or will be) in that business.
- It helps us look outside the business (or new venture) to better understand the *opportunities* and *threats* in the environment in which we operate (or will operate).
- It helps us look inside the business (or new venture) to identify our current or potential *strengths* and *weaknesses*.
- It helps us use our strengths to take advantage of market opportunities while minimizing our weaknesses and the impact of outside threats.

Even if you are entering solo practice, taking time to address the above-mentioned topics is essential. If you are sharing your venture with others—even one other partner—the process becomes more complex and is a *business imperative*. The following paragraphs are written to facilitate planning for a small medical group setting.

Often, when there is a new venture or significant organizational change, a call is placed to a local attorney who is asked to draw boxes and develop a legal structure to accommodate vague objectives. An appropriate legal structure is critical, but it should not short-circuit the planning process. In fact, the legal structure should be one of the last issues addressed in planning for the business. A common saying in planning circles is "form follows function." In other words, make decisions about your business—and about your role in that business—then build the legal structure to facilitate successful implementation of the plan.

The business planning process should include a series of questions thoughtfully considered by the business owner (or owners) in each of the following categories:

- **Environmental Assessment:** In Chapter One, we discussed the process of deciding where you want to practice. Once the community location decision is made, it is important for you to determine how you can best enter the community and position or place your practice for success. As mentioned earlier, if you are a primary care physician, particularly in a larger community, the geographic location of your practice will dramatically affect the population you serve, your payer mix, and your likely affiliation with a hospital and specialty physicians. It may also significantly affect your personal income. Primary care providers tend to draw a majority of their practice from a relatively short distance around their physical practice location. Patients tell us they prefer a practice within a short drive of their homes, particularly for their children's doctor. If you are a specialist, your location will likely define your preferred hospital affiliation and your primary care referral sources. Specialists may draw referrals from long distances depending on the number of competitive (same or substitute specialty) alternatives that are available in the community. Your analysis of your geographic options should include the following considerations:

  - Is the potential patient population growing in my selected practice geography, or is the population stable? Is the community vibrant and growing, with new businesses and neighborhoods?

  - Does my selected market geography have a broad range of income levels, as evidenced by homes and neighborhoods in the area?

  - Is there excess demand for my specialty, or are there already enough physicians in my area of expertise? Who are my competitors, and where are they located? (Ask potential referral sources and others in your field.)

  - Is my potential affiliated hospital growing and emphasizing my specialty as a service line? Is the hospital a magnet for my patients and specialty?

  - How successful are the physicians who have started practice in the area during the past three to five years?

Obviously, the ideal geography for a new practice is one that includes a growing population, a good mix of middle- and higher-income households, and a real need for your specialty.

- **Mission, Vision, and Values:** Identifying and documenting a common mission, vision, and values among the owners, the principals, or the key contributors to the practice is a critical first step in the planning process. There is much debate about mission statements and value propositions, but four fundamental issues should be addressed during this phase of the planning process:

- Identify your fundamental purpose in building a practice.
- Document your philosophy of clinical care and patient/customer service.
- Describe what you hope to achieve over the next three to five years (back to your ideal practice setting).
- Identify the values you would like to motivate your behavior and the behavior of your employees.

  Do your partners and business associates share your vision? If not, stop the process until a shared mission, vision, and values can be established, or seek new partners.

- **Governance:** In small business, "governance" usually defines the process for setting direction and making decisions. This section of the plan defines or documents who sets the direction for the practice and who establishes the policies to be followed, and it clarifies who can obligate the practice (sign contracts). Obviously, in a solo practice setting, the owner/entrepreneur is the governor, and the decision-making process is relatively clear. As soon as a second partner is added, however, the concepts of governance become much more complex. Sharing these responsibilities might include the following questions:

  - Will all the partners be decision makers with equal authority?
  - Will group decisions require consensus, or will the majority rule? What happens if no clear majority exists (e.g., two partners who disagree)? Will arbitration be part of the decision-making process?
  - Will the group hire a manager, and will that person play a role in governance?
  - How often will the governing body meet?
  - How, and how often, will the decision makers pause to plan for the future?
  - How will the group handle an impaired partner?
  - How will new members enter the group, and how will established members exit?

  The process of planning can help the partners learn to make joint decisions based on correct principles rather than private agendas.

- **Practice Development:** Like each of these sections, practice development could fill an entire volume. Developing a solo or group medical practice includes defining the services you will offer, identifying those to whom you will offer your services (including patients and referring physicians), delineating your pricing for the services, and defining how you will deliver those services. Importantly, practice development also includes how you educate or promote your services to your target customers. Terms like *marketing*, *advertising*, and *selling* have sometimes been avoided by the professions, but the success of any medical practice is dependent on the "customer" having a clear understanding of your availability and services. A few key planning questions to consider under this section include:

  - What will be the scope of services we offer in our practice? Do we have any special areas of interest or distinctive competencies that will differentiate us from our competitors? Will we offer basic laboratory, radiology, or other diagnostic tests?
  - What geographic area (or areas) will provide the majority of our business? How many potential customers are included in that area?

- What growth barriers exist in our defined geographic market, and how can we overcome those barriers? (Even professionals must realize that every similar or alternative practice is a potential competitor.)
- What is our commitment to customer service, and how will we make that commitment a reality in every aspect of our practice with every patient/customer and every referral source?
- What promotional techniques will best educate potential customers and referral sources about our service offerings?

- **Human Resources:** The most valuable resource in any organization is the human resource. Regardless of how competent you may be as a physician, your support staff will enhance or limit the growth and profitability of your medical practice. Both patients and referring physicians (and their office staff members) will likely have far more interaction with your staff members than with you. Hiring the best people you can find, for the wages you can afford, is essential. Before you hire, however, a number of questions need to be answered as part of your planning process:

  - Will group physicians practice with an employment contract or a partnership agreement? Will that agreement include a covenant not to compete if one physician decides to leave the practice?
  - Will we hire or engage part-time physicians? Will we hire or engage two part-time physicians in a job-share arrangement? (In our experience, part-time practice is not usually financially viable, particularly in the cognitive specialties. Sharing a single practice between two physicians using the same office, examination rooms, and staff, however, can work.)
  - What job positions and job skills will be required to help us accomplish our mission and provide the services we intend to offer?
  - How will the tasks and skills be divided among specific positions as documented in job descriptions?
  - How will we set wage ranges for each job position? How, and how often, will we update those wage ranges?
  - What benefits will we offer our employees, such as health insurance, time off, retirement contributions, and so on?
  - How will we document and appraise employee performance?

- **Operations:** This section describes how you will conduct your daily business. Operating policies and procedures are usually the major focus of discussion. Among the factors that planners should consider are the following:

  - *Organization Chart:* How will the jobs be organized to ensure the "highest and best use" of each human resource (e.g., physicians do what only physicians can do and delegate the rest)?
  - *Process Flow:* How will we ensure that each step in the patient visit is efficient and effective while contributing to a positive overall experience for the patient? Steps to consider include:
    - Appointment scheduling
    - Reception
    - Reception room
    - Clinical assistant handoff and patient work-up
    - Examination room wait
    - Physician examination

- Ancillary services
- Patient education
- Specialty or diagnostic referral
- Cashier
- Return visit schedule
- Billing

- *Medical Records:* How will medical records be formatted? Will we dictate or handwrite our progress notes? How quickly must the records be completed? Will physicians in our group be required to do their own procedure coding? How often will our documentation and coding be reviewed for adequacy?

- *Vendor Selection and Purchasing*: How will we determine our preferred vendors? Will we establish stock levels for key medical supplies? Will we allow vendors to stock our shelves to predetermined levels? Who will be authorized to order clinical and office supplies and at what levels? Will we participate in group purchasing contracts?

- *Quality Assurance:* How will we ensure that our patients receive quality clinical care in a caring environment? How will we measure the clinical quality and the service quality of our medical practice? How will we document and manage untoward events? How will we manage malpractice risk?

- *Productivity Targets:* Will we establish minimum productivity targets for physicians to ensure the financial viability of the practice? How will we accommodate different styles of practice and different approaches to the practice of medicine? How will we document those style differences in the appointment schedule so that the schedule maximizes the productivity of each physician? Will we double book our schedule to compensate for "no shows" (those who miss appointments)?

- *Call Coverage:* What will be our call coverage arrangements? How will we ensure that our call coverage group or network fosters the same standards of clinical and service quality that we espouse in our practice?

- *Accounts Receivable Management:* How will we emphasize the role of the receptionist to verify patient data and to collect cash at the point of service? How will we measure the success of these efforts? Will we process insurance claims internally or through a vendor? Who will manage patient due balances and past due accounts?

- **Management Information System:** Management information has become increasingly critical, complex, and costly in medical practice, particularly as practices work toward implementing an electronic medical record. It therefore is a topic worthy of serious consideration in the planning process for a solo or group practice. Computer software and hardware are certainly critical to any discussion of management information, but these are only tools to facilitate clinical and business decision making, accounts receivable management, and business processes. The development of a management information system in a practice should start with a detailed listing of all the functions required to achieve your vision, to measure your performance, to support medical decision making, and to manage practice operations. Once the functional list is developed, procedures and software can be identified to support the functions. This is discussed more fully in Chapter Five.

- **Accounting:** No physician would practice medicine in this day and age without utilizing diagnostic tools to enhance a physical examination when appropriate. Failure to do so would be considered reckless. Likewise, failure to obtain and review frequent diagnostic reports on the business of your medical practice is foolish at best. Establishing a relationship with a bookkeeper and/or accountant will be an important step in implementing your practice plans. We strongly recommend an accountant that uses the same (or similar) general ledger definitions as the Medical Group Management Association or the American Medical Group Association; this will facilitate the important process of benchmarking your practice with outside performance indicators.

Accounting supports several critical objectives in a medical practice. One is to support the allocation of overhead expenses, particularly as it affects the compensation of physicians in the group. Another is to measure practice financial and statistical performance to compare that performance both over time and with outside benchmarks.

If you are entering solo practice, this phase of the planning process will focus on performance measurement. If you are forming a group practice, the allocation of overhead and physician compensation will be a significant part of your discussion. Planning for overhead allocation usually involves three types of expenses: fixed expenses, variable expenses, and direct expenses. A description of each type follows:

Expense Type	Common Allocation
Direct Expenses: Expenses directly attributable to a single physician and not enjoyed by any other member of the group (e.g., high-end mobile phone and extra clinical assistant).	These expenses are charged directly to the individual physician.
Variable Expenses: Expenses that vary with the volume of patients seen (e.g., clinical supplies, outside transcription, and outside billing costs).	These expenses are shared according to a percentage of some measure of productivity (e.g., patient visits, work relative value units, and net revenue).
Fixed Expenses: Expenses that are incurred by the group and do not vary with patient volume over the short term (e.g., building occupancy and most support staff).	These expenses are shared equally by the practicing partners.

Generally, for compensation, benefits, and retirement, physician partners will receive the amount that is left after expenses (less any cash reserve amounts) are allocated to each physician's collections. This methodology maintains physician motivation and avoids having the higher producers subsidize the lower producers.

In addition to clarifying how overhead will be allocated and the physician or physicians will be compensated, your planning process should include a review of the diagnostic tools available for the business and the ratios, statistics, and benchmarks critical to your practice situation and your specialty. Every practice should produce (or have a bookkeeper or accountant produce) an income statement (profit and loss) on a monthly basis. This statement can be produced on a "cash" or an "accrual" basis. Cash-basis accounting is usually adequate for a small practice and uses collected dollars minus expenses actually paid as the measure of profit or loss each month. Accrual accounting is a more sophisticated method in which revenue is defined as billed charges less anticipated contractual allowances (the portion of your fees that Medicare and other payers will not pay). Expenses are allocated based on when they are incurred rather than when they are paid. Your accountant can help you to decide which approach is best for your practice.

A statement of assets and liabilities (a balance sheet) should be developed by your accountant and reviewed at least quarterly. This financial report helps business owners to understand the general health of their business by comparing their assets, liabilities, and owner's equity.

It is always good to compare your practice performance over time (e.g., month to month) to ensure that performance trends are moving you toward your objectives. It is also very useful to maintain perspective by comparing your performance with outside benchmarks for similar practices in your specialty. This benchmark comparison is most easily accomplished by calculating performance ratios and then comparing them with information available through the Medical Group Management Association, American Medical Group Association, or similar database. Some common performance statistics and ratios follow (*Note:* In calculating the ratios, use Net Patient Revenue (NPR) if your practice will use accrual accounting; use Collections if your practice will use cash basis accounting):

Performance Indicator	Calculation
New Patient Ratio: Indicates the underlying growth of a primary care practice.	New Patient Visits/Total Visits
Collection Ratio: Indicates the percentage of billed charges collected. (We recommend at least a three-month moving average.)	(NPR or Collections)/Gross Charges
Physician Expense Ratio: Indicates the percentage of physician expense.	Physician W-2 Compensation and Benefits/(NPR or Collections)
Support Staff Labor Ratio: Indicates the percentage of nonphysician support staff expense.	Support Staff compensation and Benefits/(NPR or Collections)
Building Occupancy Ratio: Measures the cost of lease and utilities as a percentage of net patient revenue or collections.	Building Costs/(NPR or Collections)
Clinical Supply Ratio: Indicates clinical supply costs as a percentage of NPR or collections.	Clinical Supply Cost/(NPR or Collections)
Coding Index: An indicator of coding performance for each physician or mid-level provider.	Work Relative Value Units/Patient Visits

- **Finance:** The finance section of your planning process will help to define your financial requirements for the new practice. You will need money, or *investment capital,* for assets like medical equipment, office equipment, furnishings, computer system, and so on. You will also need *operating capital* to pay yourself, to meet the payroll for your support staff, to pay rent, to purchase clinical supplies and office supplies, and so forth. It can take primary care practices two years or more before they consistently reach break-even operations (cash collected covers expenses incurred). Specialty practices can reach break-even operations more quickly but still need several months of operating capital while patient volume increases and to fund the practice while you wait to be paid for the services you have rendered. The delay between the date of service and payment creates the accounts receivable. A detailed pro forma financial statement helps to estimate your operating capital needs, which may be tens of thousands of dollars.

■ **Legal Structure:** As the business planning process nears completion and your vision and operations are clarified, you are in a position to discuss your legal organization with a qualified attorney. A qualified attorney will be interested in understanding your vision, your business objectives, and your operating structure. He or she will then recommend the legal structure that will best facilitate your success while minimizing risk to you and your assets. Make sure you check with other physicians in the community to find an attorney with health care experience.

FINANCING OPTIONS

The business planning process we discussed in the previous section is a critical component of the financing process. As mentioned earlier, a business plan should identify the amount of investment capital and operating capital that will be required to accomplish your business objectives. With the planning process completed, you are prepared to consider options to fund or finance the plan.

An old rule of thumb in business goes something like this: "Starting a business takes twice as long and costs twice as much as anticipated." Those starting medical practices should take heed of this counsel. One of the most common reasons for business failure is lack of adequate capital. As mentioned earlier, capital is the money needed to fund the purchase of furnishings and equipment and to finance practice operations until cash flow can consistently support a biweekly payroll and other operating expenses. The time to secure adequate financing is before the practice starts rather than waiting until the practice is in desperate straits because of short financing.

New practices have two common sources of financing. The first is a local hospital, which may be able to demonstrate a need for your specialty in the communities it serves. The second is a bank or similar financial institution, which has a small business or commercial loan department. We will briefly discuss each of these options.

The Hospital as a Financier

Nonprofit hospitals avoid the payment of certain taxes because of their commitment to a charitable purpose, usually providing care to all community members regardless of their ability to pay. These entities in particular have to be concerned about how they use their tax-exempt dollars, especially in situations where those dollars might benefit a private individual or organization. Hospitals must be able to demonstrate the value of their capital investment in projects that will further their tax-exempt purpose and mission of meeting the health care needs of the communities they serve. They must also demonstrate they have paid or received "fair market value" for their investments in organizations and people. The financial relationships between hospitals and physicians have come under increasing scrutiny during the past several years, with heavy consequences for *both* parties if federal or state agencies suspect (or actually find) inappropriate dealings.

The lifeblood of any hospital is its affiliated medical staff. Executives, physician leaders, and even board members will often participate in formal medical staff development planning to ensure that adequate numbers of primary care and specialty physicians are recruited and are successful in their practices. Determining the adequacy of physician supply involves comparing current community need for specific specialties with the actual number of physicians currently practicing. If there is a clearly demonstrable community need, hospitals can assist new physicians to meet that need through income guarantees and start-up loans that may even include "loan forgiveness" in exchange for the physician remaining in the community over a period of time.

An income guarantee helps to ensure that practice expenses can be paid and that a new physician will enjoy an adequate income while a new practice grows. "Adequate income" is usually defined as the fair market value for a particular physician specialty in the local or regional marketplace. Fair market value may be determined by using comparables such as offers made by competitors or a database such as Medical Group Management Association survey results.

Once fair compensation is determined, an income guarantee usually involves the hospital comparing the monthly cash flow in a new practice with the actual overhead expenses to see what, if anything, is left for the physician's income. The hospital will then make up the difference by providing cash to fund any operating shortfall and the physician's personal compensation according to the agreement. The cash provided by the hospital becomes a loan to the physician and the practice, and it will bear an interest rate that is, again, fair market value. Often, that loan and the accompanying interest will be forgiven if the physician remains in the community for a certain number or years (in our experience, three to five years is not uncommon). A portion of the loan and interest is frequently forgiven for each year served. Failure to remain in the community usually requires that the loan and interest (at least those portions that have not been forgiven) be paid back to the hospital. Make sure you work with your tax advisor, because you will likely have personal tax implications for any loan amounts that are forgiven.

The length of an income guarantee period often depends on the physician specialty and the practice situation. Most guarantees for primary care practices extend over two years, the approximate time to properly "grow" a primary care practice from scratch. Specialty practice income guarantees, however, particularly for invasive specialists, may be as short as a year, because surgical practices tend to produce more cash more quickly.

The advantages of an income guarantee are clear. The income guarantee offers a significant advantage over most other forms of financing for new medical practices. The prudent physician, however, will also consider the underlying market area and specific location dynamics of the practice opportunity to ensure the new practice has a high likelihood for success after the income guarantee period has expired.

A Banking Relationship

Regardless of your circumstances and your relationship with a hospital, you will need to develop a relationship with a local bank. That relationship will include both frequent transactions, such as bank deposits and withdrawals, as well as potential business loans or lines of credit. Again, the time to create these banking relationships is before they are needed.

It is not unusual for a small business to have a line of credit to assist in times of slower cash flow or to provide cash for additional capital needs, anticipated or otherwise. A line of credit is a bank's commitment to loan you up to a certain dollar amount on demand. If cash is running tight, for example, you may transfer monies from your line of credit to your checking account to make the payroll or pay other operating expenses. You only pay interest on the amount of money you borrow for the time it is outstanding. A line of credit assumes that you will make minimum payments of interest and principle that will vary depending on the portion of the credit line used. Most businesses will pay down their credit lines during times of strong cash flow so they have additional opportunity to draw on those lines during tight times. A line of credit will often be secured by home equity or a business asset, such as accounts receivable. For small businesses, the interest rate charged on outstanding credit line balances will often range between one and three points above the prime lending rate.

Banks will also make traditional commercial loans for tangible assets, such as furnishings or equipment. As opposed to an on-demand credit line, these loans are usually offered for a specific purpose and a defined timeframe. They are often collateralized or secured by the assets themselves and require regular monthly payments of fixed principle and interest. Make sure your commercial loan does not contain any penalty for prepayment so that you can eliminate the debt as your cash flow strengthens. Once again, these loans will have interest rates ranging between one and three percentage points above the prime lending rate.

Most banks have a commercial loan officer or small business-lending expert who can provide guidance and serve as an advocate for small business owners. While your medical training will provide some legitimacy to your loan application, you should be prepared to present a written description of your vision for your medical practice and how you will make it successful. A simple business plan (discussed earlier) will also help to legitimize your application. In addition, it is important to provide a pro forma financial statement (a projection of revenues and expenses) that demonstrates the sources and uses of cash to fund the start-up and operations of your fledgling practice. Again, the right loan officer can assist you through this process and help you provide the information needed to pass the scrutiny of the bank's loan committee, which usually must approve all loans. Your hospital contacts, an accountant, or other consultant can also provide valuable assistance in this process.

Equipment Leasing

An alternative to traditional debt for asset acquisition is a leasing option. Banks and other financing companies will often lease equipment to small businesses, including medical practices. Like a bank loan, a lease is often secured by the equipment it finances. Frequently, leases will come with a lower monthly payment than a bank loan but have a large buyout at the end of the lease period if you want to keep the equipment. A lease may be a useful tool during the early months of a medical practice, when cash flow is at a minimum. It is important to remember, however, that a lease is still debt and obligates the borrower to monthly payments, just like a commercial loan.

Vendors will often lease (or arrange a lease for) equipment or furnishings to medical practices. Many of these leases are legitimate and might be carefully considered as part of your financing package. Remember, however, that some equipment may require expensive supplies, such as reagents or ink, that should be included in the overall lease/purchase decision.

Bank loans, lines of credit, leases, and other forms of financing are necessary tools for establishing a new medical practice. They should be treated with tremendous caution, however, and be used judiciously. It has been said that debt (and the accompanying interest) is a master that never sleeps and never takes a vacation or a weekend off. The wise physician will enter into debt carefully and eliminate that debt quickly. The safest and least expensive form of financing is always your own money. Consequently, you should always save a portion of your income to create a pool of investment capital, over time, on which you can draw to meet the needs of your business. Consult your tax advisor to help determine the best way to accumulate or reserve capital given the legal/tax structure of your practice.

ARE YOU PROTECTED?

A critical component of your business plan should be the protection of your personal and business assets. The following section highlights several considerations and options for acquiring that protection.

The Malpractice Dilemma

Depending on your specialty, medical malpractice insurance may be one of the highest practice operating costs you will incur on an annual basis. It is also one of the wisest investments to protect your personal and medical practice assets. Even the most clinically competent of physicians is potentially vulnerable to a malpractice claim—legitimate or not. In recent years, an increasingly litigious society has made insuring against this business risk paramount. Some states allow physicians to practice without malpractice insurance coverage, but we strongly discourage "going bare." A malpractice claim is an increasingly likely event during a physician's career, and it only takes one to devastate, both financially and emotionally, even the most successful physician and his or her practice.

It is important to note that malpractice insurance is regulated at the state level and, therefore, may differ from state to state, as will the malpractice risk environment. It is also critical to note that malpractice claims, settlements, and judgments in some states have driven up insurance premiums to the breaking point, causing an exodus of physicians and/or increasing the employment of specialists by hospitals striving to maintain their service lines. When contemplating a practice location, be sure to identify the current malpractice situation as a decision factor. Nearly every state requires that a physician maintain medical malpractice liability coverage. In addition, most health care facilities require certain minimum coverage levels for those physicians applying for medical staff privileges. Your medical specialty will also play a significant factor in the cost and availability of malpractice insurance in certain areas of the country.

The following paragraphs will provide some basic understanding of the insurance products available, but they will not eliminate the need for you to thoroughly research the carriers, products, and regulatory issues in the area where you wish to establish your practice.

Coverage Options

Two common options are available for malpractice insurance coverage, although they are not necessarily available in every state. These options are claims-made and occurrence policies, each of which will be briefly described below.

The most common type of professional liability insurance purchased today is claims-made coverage. *Claims-made coverage* is defined as a policy providing protection for claims that occur and are reported while the policy is in effect (sometimes called the "coverage period"). Under a claims-made policy, the critical factor in determining coverage for a claim is the date the claim is filed. This option allows a new provider to obtain this insurance at a relatively low cost in the first few years of practicing medicine, when the risk of a claim is still relatively low because of limited exposure and the usual length of time between an occurrence of malpractice and the filing of a claim. An insurance carrier will increase the lower initial premiums in steps over the first five to seven years of practice as the number of patient encounters (the exposure) increases. In our experience, premiums will then level off for physicians who stay with the same carrier over time unless significant claims or regulatory changes occur. Because of the nature of a claims-made policy, your claims history is one of the most significant factors in determining your premium.

When choosing a claims-made policy, it is important to understand the impact of this option on termination of the coverage. Keep in mind that your claims-made policy will only cover you for claims that have been filed *during* the coverage period that relate to services rendered during that period. If you leave the carrier for any reason, you could be personally liable for additional claims that might surface after the coverage period has ended unless you invest in a supplemental policy, such as tail coverage and prior-acts (also called retroactive or nose) coverage. *Tail coverage* is a supplemental insurance policy covering incidents that occurred during the "active" (or coverage) period of a claims-made policy but were not filed before termination of the coverage. Typically, tail coverage is purchased from your *previous* claims-made carrier, and costs range from 125% to 250% of the prior year's premium, so it can be a substantial investment. *Prior-acts coverage* is a supplemental policy purchased from the *new* carrier to cover claims filed for services rendered before the effective date of a new malpractice insurance policy and after the retroactive date of that policy. Again, supplemental coverage is expensive, a fact that should be considered as part of the claims-made insurance decision. Even employed physicians should make sure that tail coverage on a claims-made policy is provided by the employer before signing an employment contract.

Another form of malpractice insurance coverage is an occurrence policy. An *occurrence policy* will provide insurance coverage for any incident that occurs while the policy is in effect, regardless of when the claim is actually filed. By its nature, an occurrence policy insures you against malpractice claims whenever they occur after the policy becomes effective, so the occurrence option will typically have a higher annual premium. The higher premium, however, eliminates the need to purchase a supplemental policy on termination of the insurance.

Because of a variety of circumstances, including how often you change carriers, it is difficult to say which type of malpractice insurance option is best in terms of overall costs. The claims-made option is increasingly appealing to many new physicians simply because of the lower cash commitment during the early years.

Insurance Carrier Considerations

When deciding on the type of policy that best suits your needs, it is also good business to consider the rendering carrier. Several times during the past ten years, malpractice insurance companies have filed for bankruptcy and have been liquidated. Ask physicians who have been through this liability exposure and settlement process, and they will confirm the need to be vigilant about the malpractice insurance carrier you select. Recently, some insurance carriers have simply opted to discontinue providing malpractice insurance as a product line because of the increasing risk of litigation. One way to identify an insurance company with solid performance is to use the insurance ratings provided by AM Best Company, Inc., which are recognized as reliable industry benchmarks (http://www.ambest.com/ratings/default.asp). The ratings take into consideration the insurer's financial position based on a review of the company's financial statements, including their balance sheet and operating performance. Look for companies that have a B++ to A++ rating.[1]

Many commercial carriers are for-profit companies owned by shareholders whose desires for stock performance can influence the company's strategy and tactics. In an attempt to better represent physicians and keep malpractice premiums in check, some doctors have formed physician mutual companies. A *physician mutual company* is an insurance carrier owned by its physician policyholders. These physician-owned companies are dedicated to providing reliable malpractice coverage for their members at affordable rates. Physician mutual companies are typically state-based and provide coverage to a large number office-based physicians.

---

[1]David R. Deardon, JD and Michael R. Burke, JD. Do you have the right Malpractice Insurance? Family Practice Management Vol. 2 Issue 10 http://doctor.medscape.com/viewarticle/49489/

Policy Coverage and Exclusions

Policy coverage and exclusions are additional factors to consider when comparing policy options and premiums. Not all malpractice insurance policies are created equal. Consequently, comparing carriers should also include a review of the terms and conditions detailed in a sample policy. Many policies exclude coverage for certain claims involving punitive damages, intentional misconduct, or other exclusions. Review the "consent to settle" provisions that define the terms under which you and the carrier will settle instead of litigate a claim. Remember that every settled claim is a paid claim and will affect your premium ratings for the rest of your career. As you complete your insurance application, make sure that you provide honest and complete responses to the carrier's inquiries. Failure to do so may provide the carrier with reason not to cover a claim if research shows you have withheld or misrepresented information that was material to their decision to insure you. Full disclosure is the safest route. As always, it is prudent to consult experienced legal counsel regarding all contracts, including malpractice coverage, before making your decision. You may not be able to change standard agreements provided by certain carriers, but you will never know unless you ask. Regardless, your legal advisor will help you better understand the pros and cons of each policy beyond the premium amounts.

Depending on the state in which you practice, there may be other coverage requirements and surcharges that will influence your protection and your cost of coverage. Make sure your research into practice locations also includes a discussion of patient compensation funds, joint underwriting associations, and other state-mandated options.

Protecting Your Business

In addition to malpractice insurance, those physicians entering private practice will want to consider several other types of insurance against business risk. Common types of business insurance (excluding those associated with your employees and their benefits, which will be discussed in Chapter Six) and their general application include:

Insurance Type	Application
Property Insurance	Insuring against the risk of significant untoward events (e.g., fire and burglary) is an important consideration depending on the level of investment you have made in your property and equipment. Property insurance is, in our experience, the most common business insurance investment among medical practices.
General Liability Insurance	General liability insurance protects the business against injury or accident claims (e.g., someone slipping on the ice outside your office) and a variety of other potential lawsuits (frivolous or otherwise).
Professional Liability Insurance	Depending on the legal structure of your practice, professional liability insurance to protect your business assets may be an important consideration. Business liability policies will protect your business in case of a lawsuit and may even pay legal fees to defend your business assets.

Continued

Continued

Insurance Type	Application
Business Disruption Insurance	If your practice is disrupted by a significant untoward event that lasts more than a few days (e.g., Hurricane Katrina), having coverage to continue paying the bills could be critical to your survival. Several natural disasters in recent years have increased the popularity of business disruption insurance in some settings. Business disruption insurance can offset a portion of your lost revenue while you rebuild, restore, or relocate a damaged business. Business disruption insurance is frequently an additional rider on property insurance policies and may be worth considering, particularly in some geographic areas.
Product Liability Insurance	If your practice sells a product, you may want to consider product liability insurance, which protects the business if someone is harmed by your product. Products such as vitamins, eyewear, and other medical devices, if sold by your practice, might make you vulnerable to product liability.
Key Employee Insurance (Key "Man" Insurance)	Key employee policies are available to protect business from the loss of a key person within the company. If you are a sole proprietor, such insurance may not be necessary. In a partnership or group practice, however, insuring the lives of key revenue producers may be a wise investment. Premiums for such policies are paid by the business, which is also the beneficiary. Such policies may be a boon to a group practice that loses a busy provider to illness or accident and must recruit a replacement.
Employment Practices Liability Insurance	In today's increasingly litigious society, it is not uncommon for employees who feel their personal legal rights have been violated to sue an employer for damages. Employment practices liability insurance helps to protect the business in the event of claims like sexual harassment, wrongful termination, discrimination, and others. Typically, larger companies with many employees (and higher exposure) will purchase this insurance, but it may be worth considering for smaller organizations as well. Some liability carriers will offer some limited protection as part of a larger liability policy, but it is also available as a stand-alone product.
Disability Insurance	This protects you from income disruption because of a long-term illness or severe injury. (Disability insurance will be discussed in detail in Chapter Six.)

Seek the advice of your accountant, attorney, or other consultants when considering your exposure as a business owner. These experts will be able to provide information regarding local regulatory requirements and the routine types of coverage needed to protect you and your business. Some liability insurance carriers will offer a Business Owners Policy, which includes coverage for a variety of common risks faced by small business. Such bundling may result in premium dollar savings versus purchasing several separate policies.

One important area for medical practice owners to consider is a dishonest employee. An unfortunate reality of hiring people is the potential for hiring someone who will steal from the practice. Even small monetary amounts can add up to big dollars over time. Proper internal accounting controls can help to mitigate the opportunity for theft, but for those with the mindset to steal, creative schemes continue to surface. Fidelity bonds offer protection against the results of theft, embezzlement, and forgery. The bond can be associated with specific positions in your office or can cover the entire business. Fidelity bonds can often be purchased as part of a business liability coverage bundle (mentioned earlier) or as an individual policy. You may consider covering specific areas of your business where individuals have access to money.

CHAPTER SUMMARY

In this chapter, we have talked about planning how you will be in the business of medicine, how you can obtain the money necessary to fund your business venture, and how you can protect yourself and your medical practice in this litigious age. Each of these topics will require your time and energy to help ensure that you make correct decisions. Once again, your investment of time here is relatively minor compared to your clinical training. Properly planning, financing, and protecting your business can help to ensure that you have the opportunity to practice your clinical profession while avoiding the horror stories of failed practices and partnerships.

CHAPTER Three

FACILITY AND SITE SELECTION

SHOULD I LEASE OR BUY?

Once you have identified the community where you want to practice and the general area within that community where you want to locate your office, you are ready to move on to the next important location step.

Within a given area, there may be a dozen possible locations to lease or buy space for your office. Generally speaking, the answer to the "lease versus buy" question for *new* practice office space is "don't buy"—generally speaking. There may be a rare opportunity out there that you just cannot pass up (check in with your personal investment and tax advisors), but generally, new physicians have enough debt and risk without becoming property owners.

Why not buy? First, you may not have the money to buy property and prepare it for use. The money you do have is probably needed elsewhere at this point in your career. Second, even with the best analysis, you may choose a practice site or situation that turns out to be less than you had hoped. Third, over time, your practice location may become less desirable. The neighborhood may change in terms of population demographics or commercial ventures. Finally, your "loyalties" may shift, or you may find it desirable to change geographic locations to take advantage of new opportunities. Regardless, a short-term lease will provide you additional flexibility not found in a mortgage. Having to lease or dispose of your property while paying rent in a new location would be difficult for the best of practices.

For example, one of our clients merged his practice with several other physicians to create a very competitive, new, single-specialty group. The office he owned was too small, too old, and poorly positioned to accommodate the new group, so they selected a more appropriate space on the other side of town. Unfortunately, this wonderful new opportunity left the physician owning space in an old building that he could not lease or sell. His investment became a millstone. Despite needing to take advantage of this new opportunity, he was still paying a mortgage, owner's association fees, and property taxes. Fortunately, he had been in practice for many years and could tolerate the expense. Had he been out of residency only a few years, however, that extra financial burden may have been unbearable.

So, we will assume that you are going to lease—at least to start your practice.

As a new physician, you will likely have a busy start-up schedule and little time for wandering around town looking for a place to hang your shingle. You may also be relocating to a community far from the area where you complete your training. If so, you may find that a commercial real estate agent can be a tremendous help in locating space. Within defined parameters, the agent can scout out the options quickly and, fortunately for you, free of charge. A commercial agent will be able to provide a summary of possible locations and initial terms being offered by their owners.

The agent will need your property preferences. These will include your chosen geographic parameters, the square footage you will need, how you will use the space, and the amount of rent you are willing or able to pay each month. Your commercial realtor will help you to decide the amount of tenant improvement money you should attempt to negotiate to build out your space (tenant improvement allowance will be discussed shortly). Your agent will then provide a document showing possible locations based on your search parameters and will facilitate your site visits to selected locations.

When you choose a commercial realtor, it is important to remember some state laws stipulate that the agent ultimately works for the building owner, not for you. Because the owner is paying the commission, the agent has a fiduciary responsibility to the owner. Bear this fact in mind as you review lease terms with the agent. In other states, the laws require that even though the agent is paid by the owner, he or she still works for you and will try to get you the best deal possible. You need to be aware of who the agent is representing, so ask. The agent should have no problem disclosing the responsibilities and obligations he has to you and to the owner.

If you begin working with an agent and find you are not comfortable with that individual, you have every right to find another agent with whom you can work more comfortably. Let the first agent know you feel that a change is necessary, and do not be intimidated by a negative response. If you ultimately choose a location presented by the first agent, he or she will be entitled to a portion of the commission. Otherwise, you are not obligated to that first agent.

Depending on your circumstances, you may have more time to work on space selection. For example, if you are starting practice in the community where you will complete your training, you may be able to devote more time to hunting for an office. Recently, in finding an office for a specialist, we did not use a commercial real estate agent. The selected space was a large, multistory building with its own lease management company. Because we saved the owner the commission expense, we were able to negotiate an increase in the tenant improvement allowance without increasing the rent. You are under no obligation to use an agent if you have the time and the inclination to work through the site selection process yourself.

Depending on the sophistication of your new landlord, the lease documents presented to you for signature may be well thought out and standardized, or they may be barely legible copies of copies. In either case, you can assume that the lease will be biased toward the building owner. Even when there is support from a commercial realtor, we always recommend that our physician clients consult competent legal counsel before signing a lease. Your attorney is your agent and receives no commission on the deal. Yes, there will be some legal fees involved, but the pain and agony that accompany signing a bad lease go well beyond a few thousand dollars in initial fees. We will discuss a few key lease terms later in this chapter.

I HAVE FOUND THE SPACE, NOW WHAT?

Although you have found that perfect site, on that perfect corner in a great building, you will likely need to make some changes to the physical layout of the office you have chosen. Even if the space was previously leased to a physician, you may still need or want to make some cosmetic changes or a "face-lift," including paint or wallpaper and carpet.

Entire books have been written and college degrees awarded in architecture, design, and construction management. All we can provide here is an overview of what you can expect to encounter during a construction project. Throughout the building process, you will need the services of an architect, a contractor, and possibly, a consultant to help you.

If the space has never been "built out," which means the space is little more than a shell with a concrete floor and exterior walls, you will certainly need the services of an architect. Often, the building owner will have an architect he can recommend, and in some instances, the building owner may even require you to use his architect. Make sure you know what the lease requires before you sign.

The architect will need a document commonly referred to as a "space program." A space program tells the architect what furnishings and equipment will be located in each room, how large you would like each space to be, and what activities will occur in each room. Exhibit 3a is a sample space program that you can use as a starting point in this process. (We will discuss space planning for furnishings and equipment in Chapter Eight.) The architect can also help you develop your space program.

Like most professionals, architects are likely to be working on multiple projects simultaneously. Make sure you work with your architect to set expectations and reasonable deadlines for completing each step in the process. This will help to ensure that your project moves forward.

As you proceed with the architectural drawings, make sure that you carefully review every space, and do it more than once. The architect will not provide you with a perfect floor plan the first time (or sometimes even the third or fourth time). Envision yourself and your team working in the office. Visit other offices in your specialty, observe their office designs, and talk with the physicians and staff about what they would change if given the opportunity. If done properly, space planning is an iterative process that takes both time and patience. Use a red pencil to mark changes and questions on the plans for later review with the architect.

If you are unsure about how large a room should be or just need to verify an important space, try doing a "mock-up" of the room. Find a large area, and use masking tape to outline the *inside* edge of the room (remember that the wall may be three to four inches wide). Use additional masking tape to make outlines of the exam table, countertops, and any equipment you intend to use (or may use) in the room. This detailed process is often used in space planning for health care facilities. Several years ago, while preparing a major renovation to a hospital's intensive care unit, this process saved significant amounts of money and time by revealing errors in the assumptions that had been made regarding room size, space requirements for equipment, and nursing care issues. The time spent in planning provided a much more functional facility and eliminated many future headaches.

Changes to the plans are easy and inexpensive to make before construction begins. Once the contractor has begun working on the office, however, changes are expensive and time-consuming. Do your work on the front end of the project, and you will much happier with the end result in terms of functionality and fees!

In addition to an architect, you may want the services of an interior designer. This person will help you choose color schemes, furnishings, artwork, wall coverings, and other "finishing touches" to make your office look its best. A designer might also see problems with the floor plans that you may not have considered.

Before you choose an interior designer, make sure he or she has experience with medical offices. Ask for a sample of completed projects to visit (or at least see in a photo book). Experienced designers will be happy to show you their accomplishments. If a candidate does not have work to show, move on to someone else.

EXHIBIT 3A
****SAMPLE SPACE PROGRAM****

We Really Care Family Practice Center
Logan City Office
Space Program
Contact: Kahn Spirici, MD

Space	Size	Sq. Ft
Waiting Room (9 chairs)	16 × 16	256
Front Desk	8 × 8	64
Storage/Chart Room	10 × 10	100
Telephone & Computer Network Room	4 × 6	24
ADA Restroom	7 × 7	49
Exam Room (×3)	10 × 10	300
Procedure Room	12 × 10	120
X-Ray Suite	14 × 16	224
Physician Office	10 × 12	120
Nurse Station	8 × 10	80
Break Room	10 × 12	120
Total		1,457 (75% of Total)*
Available Square Footage		1,950

*Remember to include the industry standard 25% of total available space for hallways, walls, and utilities.

OFFICE SPACE REVIEW LIST

- Patient flow is simple and effective for such things as check-in and check-out, blood-draw station, and x-ray.
- The check-in counter is open and friendly (no windows or other barriers).
- Exam rooms are large enough to accommodate exam table, counter for writing, sink (if necessary), physician stool, two chairs, AND any equipment that may be brought into the room (e.g., EKG machine).
- At least one exam room is large enough to accommodate a wheelchair in addition to any extra equipment needed in the room. The ADA requires all rooms to be accessible, but not every room needs to have enough space to add equipment along with the wheelchair. If many of your patients require wheelchairs or other walking-assist devices, all your rooms will need to be larger.
- The procedure room is large enough to accommodate equipment used for procedures. Planning for the future is important for this space. Do you ever envision your practice purchasing a laser? How about a scope with a monitor or an ultrasound machine? A little planning today can save a lot of money down the road.
- Some, or all, of the reception counter is low enough to accommodate a person in a wheelchair.
- Is every room wired for a computer network? Even if you don't use any computers in your exam rooms today, you will probably be using them in the not-too-distant future. In some areas, you will want multiple connections available for future growth. It costs almost nothing more to pull two wires instead of one.
- If running a computer network, be sure to plan for air-conditioning in the network room (often co-located in the telephone closet room).

Some time ago, an OB/GYN we know did a cosmetic upgrade on his office. His inexperienced wife chose a wall covering that was very bright and busy, with big red flowers and vines flowing in all directions. The new wallpaper was both lovely and expensive.

Naively, she had it placed on every wall in the clinic. His pregnant patients, many in the throes of morning sickness, could not sit in the waiting room or the exam rooms without getting dizzy and nauseated. A few months later, after countless patient complaints, the doctor was forced to make an expensive change.

Several lessons can be gleaned from this doctor's experience. First, as mentioned, use an experienced interior designer. They know what works and what does not work. Second, unless you are a pediatrician, use bright colors sparingly. A conservative color scheme will make your patients feel comfortable and will be inviting and warm. Third, too much of a good thing is too much. Try to look at your office from the patient's point of view.

FINDING A CONTRACTOR AND STARTING THE CONSTRUCTION

Your architect should be able to help you solicit bids from contractors by issuing a request for proposal (RFP). An RFP is a document sent to potential contractors that outlines the project and invites them to submit a bid by a certain date. The interested contractors will be given a set of drawings and a large, spiral-bound book (commonly referred to as the "spec book," or specification book) containing specific requirements for everything in the project, including carpet, paint, lead lining for x-ray suites, ventilation, plumbing, paint color, and so on.

Try to get at least three competitive bids. As you and your architect review the incoming bids, take care to choose the best—not necessarily the lowest—bid. A contractor whose bid is significantly lower than his competitors may have missed something in his original bid. He may then try to recover some of his loss through "change orders," skimping on work and supplies, or simply walking away without finishing the job.

After accepting a bid, if you make a change to the "scope" of the project (like remembering you need to have lead lining in your x-ray suite or that you want a back door so you can sneak in and out of the office), you can expect the contractor to request a change order. Simply stated, a change order is a request to do something that was not part of the original bid submitted by the contractor. Sometimes these changes are minor (like adding a doorway) and will not cost you very much. Unfortunately, major errors like forgetting to specify lead-lined walls and doors can cost you a great deal.

Contractors salivate at the sound of a change order. A dishonest contractor may charge you much more to add a door than if the door had been in the original project bid. Additional fees may be appropriate if the contractor will have to reroute pipes and wiring to get the unplanned door in the wall. Unfortunately, it may be difficult for you to determine just how much additional cost is justified.

Avoiding change orders in a construction project is almost impossible, but you can diminish their impact. Before you send out the RFP, do a thorough review of the architectural plans and interior finishes. Have other experienced people review the plans as well. An extra set of eyes will catch things you have missed. When you think you need to make a change after the project is started, make sure you really need to make that change. Look for inexpensive alternatives to adding that door. Of course, some things just have to be done. (The forgotten lead-lined drywall has to be added if you want to use your x-ray machine.) If this is the case, then you will need to have the contractor submit a written request for a change order. The architect should do a thorough review of the change request, including getting details on the materials used (once the work is done, you have the right to request copies of invoices to verify costs). Do not pay any change request until the architect has reviewed and approved it.

Importantly, make sure all agreements or problems encountered on the project are in writing. This is essential for many reasons, including having a paper trail for your attorney.

AND SO IT BEGINS...

Once construction begins, you will want to carefully review what is happening on a regular basis. Proper oversight will require that you spend time at your new office almost daily during the first few weeks of the project. You will help to catch errors and work with the contractor and others to fix problems. For example, on the first day of a particular job, the contractor measured the distance between exam room walls incorrectly and placed door locations on the wrong side of the room. A review by the physician's consultant caught this error before the walls went up (and saved a lot of time and effort). In another project, a room designed for audiology services was too small. This error was caught after the wall framing was in place but before expensive sound insulation was installed. An adjustment was made without costing either party extra money.

During the first few weeks of construction, you will see a lot of progress being made as studs appear, plumbing is installed, and ventilation and electrical wiring are put in place. Once the drywall goes up, the progress will appear to slow considerably, however, as the seams in the drywall are covered (a process called "mudding and taping"). This is a slow process that requires drying time and more than one coat of "mud." Once the drywall is completed, everything will again appear to move very quickly as paint, wall coverings, and carpet are installed; countertops, cupboards (also known as "millwork"), and sinks are put in place; and other finishing items, such as fire alarms, finish carpentry (wood trim, if you have any in the project), and light fixtures are hung.

Construction contracts do not always include pulling wires for telephones or computer networks. If planned for early enough in the process, your electrician can pull wires for both telephone and computer networks at the same time as running other electrical wires, saving you time and money. The alternative is to have the person who sells you your telephone system/computer network install the wiring, for an additional fee, and added mess, at a later time.

PUNCH LIST

As your contractor completes the project, your careful inspection will identify items that have been missed or that need to be corrected. These items will be placed on a "punch list." Most punch lists include minor issues that were not noticed by the contractor (or that less honorable contractors were hoping you would not notice). Common punch list items may include a poor paint job, doors that are warped, wall coverings that are torn or not installed properly, cabinet doors that swing open the wrong way, or leaking faucets. Everything you see that does not meet your specifications should be corrected. Punch lists cost contractors money, generally in labor costs, so they do not like them. As an incentive, a percentage of the contractor payments (usually five percent of the total payments due) is withheld until the punch list work is completed. In addition, you should withhold another five to ten percent of the total payments due until the city or county building inspector determines the work meets building codes. Linking final payment to building permit approval creates the leverage you may need to get a contractor to properly complete his work.

On larger projects, the architect and the owner will often carry a roll of blue painter's tape. They will use the tape to show the contractor where problems exist. The contractor will prefer to solve a problem before it reaches the punch list, because it costs him less to fix a problem if his employees are still on the job.

One short note about subcontractors: Most contractors will not do all the work themselves. Because a construction project requires different skills, contractors will employ subcontractors for specialty work (e.g., electrical work or plumbing), so you will see several different companies involved on your project. (Beware, some states allow sub-contractors to sue the business owner if the contractor fails to pay them, even if the owner paid the contractor.) Regardless, the contractor is still responsible for the entire project, including paying the subcontractors.

REMODELING EXISTING SPACE

Most of the issues facing physicians who are building out an empty shell also apply to physicians who are remodeling an existing space. Depending on the complexities of the changes needed in the existing space, you may want to engage an architect. For small changes, the construction contractor may be able to accomplish the task without extensive drawings. Adding a door or moving a non-load-bearing wall is usually a simple task. An architect, however, will be needed for more complex remodeling work.

The building owner will probably have a preferred contractor for remodeling existing offices, but if you can get more than one bid, make the effort. Contractors who frequently work in a building can sometimes cost you less, because they already know the nuances and challenges of the building and do not have to guess about original construction and support systems (guessing always adds to the cost).

The steps a contractor will follow in remodeling will be much like those described previously in *New Space*. Studs, plumbing, ventilation, and electrical will be installed. Drywall will be hung, and the seams will be taped and mudded. Then, the new walls will be painted and decorated to your specifications. Even with the smallest project, oversight on your part will be necessary to ensure that the work meets your specifications. The sooner you raise questions or concerns about the work being done, the less expensive any necessary solutions will be.

PAYMENTS

The contractor will usually require a deposit (generally twenty-five percent of the total bid) once the contract is signed but before the work commences. On big projects, you should expect to get a bill every month. Smaller projects may take only a few weeks, and you may have to pay fifty percent before the contractor starts and the balance when the job is finished. Again, you should withhold five to fifteen percent of the total requested payment until all the punch list items are completed and any city/county inspector determines that the work meets building codes.

THE LEASE AGREEMENT

This section is not intended to provide legal advice. In fact, our first recommendation is that you contact a competent real estate attorney before you sign any lease for office space. This section is intended to raise your awareness of a few key items that you will likely find in a well-written lease. As you review these items, be mindful that there will always be exceptions, modifications, and unique clauses that can change the basic intent of common terms and conditions in a lease agreement. Your attorney will help guide you through the process and intricacies of lease negotiation and contracting. Make sure that you understand the following items with the help of your legal counsel:

- **Term:** The term, or length, of a lease is a primary consideration for both the lessor (the building owner) and the lessee (you). The lease term may affect the owner's ability to finance his property and will affect his willingness to contribute to tenant improvements (your build-out allowance). The term will likely affect your cost per square foot, with longer terms usually yielding a lower cost, even with cost escalators. The lease term may also affect your flexibility and your ability to renew the lease at the end of the initial term. In our experience, five-year leases are not uncommon or unreasonable for most medical practices. We prefer to see a five-year agreement with the option to renew the lease for one or more successive five-year periods. A lot can happen in five years, including significant changes in market dynamics that can affect your ability to practice. At the same time, a five-year term does allow for some amortization of reasonable build-out costs.

- **Full Service or Triple Net:** A full-service lease usually includes the costs associated with building occupancy, such as janitorial services, utilities (excluding telephone), maintenance of your space and common areas (e.g., foyers and elevators), property taxes, and so on. Alternatively, a triple-net lease requires the lessee to pay utilities associated with the leased space and contribute to common area maintenance, property taxes, and so forth. The total costs of these leases may be similar, but make sure you understand which kind of lease you are signing to properly budget for building occupancy.

- **Cost Escalators:** It is not uncommon for a landlord to place cost escalators in a lease agreement. These clauses define how your lease rate will increase over the life of the lease and should reflect anticipated inflation.

- **Common Area Maintenance:** Common area maintenance (CAM) fees are expenses that the building owner passes along to you for maintaining elevators, cleaning hallways and bathrooms, replacing carpet—anything that involves the use of the building. Usually, CAM fees are allocated to each tenant as a percentage of the total number of square feet in the building. Some owners will set the CAM expense so that it changes only once a year, based on the prior year's actual expense, but other owners will change this amount semiannually or even quarterly. Generally, CAM fees are paid each month along with the base rent. For example, the lessee of a 2,000-square-foot space that is ten percent of the rentable space in the building can expect to pay ten percent of the CAM for the building. This amount will typically be conveyed as a rate per square foot (e.g., $5.00 per square foot).

- **Leasehold Improvements:** Leasehold improvements include everything from building out a shell space to a simple remodel or face-lift for the space you will occupy. Depending on the length of the lease and other factors, many landlords will provide an allowance toward leasehold improvements (also called a build-out allowance, or a tenant improvement allowance). The allowance is usually identified as a square-foot rate and should be spelled out clearly in the lease. Some portion of the tenant improvement allowance is reflected in your overall rental rate, so the higher the allowance, the higher your monthly lease cost will be. The allowance essentially becomes an owner-financed loan to you so that you do not have to come up with all the money yourself. In offering a tenant improvement allowance, the building owner also recognizes the reality that when you leave the building at some point in the future, the walls and doors will remain, which provides a future benefit for the building owner and his next tenant. If the tenant improvement allowance will not cover all the costs of building or remodeling your office, you will either need to come up with the extra cash yourself or change your plans to match the owner's allowance.

- **Hours of Operation:** Often, you will be sharing your leased space with other tenants as opposed to leasing an entire building. Depending on how the building was constructed, you and your patients may share a common entry and exit, elevators, escalators, stairwells, and even restrooms. Modern buildings will have controls on heating and air conditioning, automatic security systems, and systems to limit lighting during evening and nighttime hours. You want to ensure that you, your staff, and your patients will have access to the building during the times you are open for practice. Make sure the hours in which the building is open will accommodate your ability to offer extended hours in the morning and evening (should you decide to do so). Make sure that there is weekend access as well.

■ **Neighbors:** You will likely have other tenants in your building or your neighborhood, so it will be useful to understand who those tenants might be and what services or products they provide. It is certainly in the landlord's best interest to rent professional space only to professionals. Your attorney can make sure your lease includes your right to operate in a quiet and appropriate setting; however, your lease cannot protect you from the practices of other landlords in other spaces nearby. City zoning regulations will usually offer some protection, but beware of the activities occurring in the neighborhood around your space.

■ **Exclusions:** There may be important exclusions in your lease agreement. Other lessees may have negotiated terms that might restrict what you can do in or with your space. The building owner may have agreements with other tenants that restrict your ability to perform certain procedures or sublet space to certain specialties. For example, a plastic surgeon may have negotiated an exclusivity clause in her lease agreement that precludes other plastic surgeons from leasing space in the building. An ear, nose, and throat group may have a clause in their lease that prevents anyone else in the building from installing a sound booth or selling hearing aids. The possibilities are only limited by the imagination of the attorneys working on previous lease agreements.

CHAPTER SUMMARY

The selection, design, and cost of your space will have a significant impact on your accessibility, your productivity, your profitability, and your quality of work life. This critical decision should be carefully considered along with the help of competent and trusted professionals. A well-chosen location and design will be attractive and convenient for patients. A sound design will ensure the proper privacy and flow of patients and will enhance your productivity and that of your office staff (see also Chapter Eight). As the third-largest cost factor in most medical practices, your building occupancy expense will significantly impact the dollars you take home as the owner of the practice. Do not skimp on the selection, planning, or implementation of your office.

CHAPTER Four

CREDENTIALING: WHAT IS IT, AND WHY DO IT?

As you begin the journey of establishing your new medical practice, you will need to examine your reimbursement options from local payer sources. Establishing relationships with the various governmental agencies and managed care organizations will include an application process referred to as *credentialing*. This process involves examining a physician's professional credentials to determine whether he or she is qualified to contract with a carrier. Most government payers and private carriers require some form of credentialing before allowing participation in their reimbursement contracts and provider panels. A similar process applies to obtaining medical staff privileges in hospitals, rehabilitation facilities, ambulatory surgery centers, and other workshops.

Not all carriers will require you to sign a contract or complete the credentialing process to receive reimbursement. So, why endure the process? Simply stated—*for the money!* There are two ways to be involved in a carrier's plan: A *participating provider* has completed a formal credentialing process and signed a contract with an insurance company for a negotiated rate of reimbursement as full payment for services rendered to patients. A *nonparticipating provider* ("*nonpar*") accepts a reduced or lower reimbursement but may have the option to bill the patient for all or part of the remaining balance.

If you choose to accept patients from a carrier but not to be a participating provider, you may place your reimbursement at risk for the following reasons:

- Some insurance carriers will send the reimbursement check to the patient rather than to a nonparticipating physician. Collecting that reimbursed amount from the patient will increase billing costs and the risks that are always associated with collecting self-pay balances.

- As an incentive to become a participating provider, carriers will often reduce reimbursement to nonparticipating physicians. Depending on the insurance plan, this reduced reimbursement can be significant (sometimes thirty percent or more). This phenomenon saddles the physician with the job of collecting a larger balance directly from the patient.

- Depending on specific carrier rules, nonparticipating physicians may only be allowed to bill a portion of the difference between what the carrier pays and the physicians' fees. Regardless of payer rules, balance billing or self-pay accounts are always the most difficult and expensive dollars for medical practices to collect.

- Importantly, some carriers may reject a claim from a nonparticipating provider, leaving a physician in the uncomfortable position of battling with the patient/customer for payment.

In short, you will likely choose to participate with most of the major providers in your community by signing a contract and submitting to their credentialing process.

Make no mistake—when you decide to participate with a payer, you are signing a contract. It is critical that you take the time to thoroughly review the terms of the contract being offered. Most governmental agreements are inflexible but fairly straightforward. The same cannot always be said for private health care insurers. Some terms are potentially confusing. We often recommend that new physicians touch base with established physicians in their own specialty regarding the performance of local payers. You should not talk about specific fees, but you should ask general questions about the perceived adequacy of reimbursement, timeliness of payment processing, and payer responsiveness to inquiries about outstanding or denied claims. Physicians and their office managers are likely sources of this information. Local billing companies may also be willing to share their experience with local payers, particularly if you are a potential customer. Because Medicare terms are relatively rigid, it may be wise to start with Medicare participation and compare other commercial carriers' terms, conditions, and reimbursement with that "standard." When an insurance carrier's local reputation and contracting language meet your needs and expectations and the fee reimbursement levels are satisfactory to you, it is usually recommended that you participate in the credentialing process to protect your bottom line.

The following paragraphs include the steps to help you begin the credentialing process.

THE CREDENTIALING PROCESS

As you begin your credentialing activities, please be aware that the process is constantly evolving. The steps detailed below were relevant at the time this manual was published, but there may be important differences when you begin to build your practice. Please consult the Centers for Medicare and Medicaid Services (CMS) website and use the search feature (http://www.cms.hhs.gov).

National Provider Identifier

Regardless of your specialty, you will need to apply for a National Provider Identifier (NPI) number. (This is formerly known as a Unique Provider Identification Number, or UPIN number.) The NPI number is issued by the CMS. This identifier is used when filing claims to indicate the physician providing the services. The CMS began to issue these numbers in 2007 to strengthen compliance with the Health Insurance Portability and Accountability Act. Federal law established that the NPI number will be used by all government and commercial or private insurance plans as the unique identifier for physician contracting and claims payment. In addition, the NPI will be used as part of the electronic health information initiatives being implemented by the CMS. For this reason, whether you plan to serve Medicare patients or not, you will need to apply for the new NPI number before you can participate with Medicare and most private insurance carriers.

The NPI application can be made online at (https://nppes.cms.hhs.gov/NPPES/Welcome.do) or by completing form CMS 10114, which is available at http://www.cms.hhs.gov/NationalProvIdentStand/03_apply.asp#TopOfPage.

Remember, the CMS can take up to 90 days to process an application for an NPI number, so the credentialing process should be started well in advance of the anticipated practice opening (we recommend 180 days). Careful review of the completed application is also recommended, because the CMS or their intermediary will return any applications with missing or incomplete data, resulting in a potential delay in your credentialing process. New providers will receive written notification of the newly issued NPI number.

Medicare Credentialing

With the exception of pediatric specialties, most physicians will likely see some Medicare patients and will want to participate in this government program to ensure the best reimbursement. Once an NPI number has been obtained, four additional steps are required to complete the Medicare Credentialing Process:

1. **Complete the Enrollment Forms:** To participate in the Medicare program, you will need to complete forms CMS 855 (the Medicare enrollment application) and CMS 460 (the Medicare Participating Physician or Supplier Agreement). Take care to obtain all of the signatures required given your practice setting, including any officer's signature as necessary. As with the NPI number, Medicare can take up to 90 days to process an application for enrollment, so the credentialing process should be initiated well in advance of the anticipated practice opening.

2. **Review Enrollment Forms:** As simple as it sounds, it is imperative that you carefully review the completed application to ensure that all necessary signatures are obtained and supporting documents are provided. Failure to provide a single signature or required document will cause the application to be returned to the physician without processing. This will delay the ability to complete other credentialing applications as well as the ability to secure reimbursement for services provided. Missing just one item can result in a returned application and the need to resubmit the forms with original signatures.

3. **Send or Deliver the Application:** We recommend that you make a complete copy of the application and all attachments before mailing or delivering the package. This copy will assist you in working with the carrier's enrollment staff should additional questions arise. Once a copy is made, we recommend a delivery option that requires the recipient's signature to verify delivery. The U.S. Postal Service and other private couriers have such options for a nominal fee.

4. **Follow Up:** Although payers will not typically release provider numbers over the telephone, it is prudent practice to make periodic contact to determine the status of your enrollment. Often, a phone call early in the process can expedite credentialing by identifying any additional information required. It is suggested that you follow up every two or three weeks until you receive the written notification of your assigned provider number or, for established providers changing practice locations, your reassignment of benefits.

It is important to remember that once you have decided to be a participating provider for Medicare, you cannot discriminate against Medicare patients or selectively accept those patients.

The Medicaid Decision and Credentialing

The Medicaid program is designed to provide medical treatment to uninsured or underinsured persons. The program is funded by both federal and state dollars and is managed at the state level. The Medicaid program typically has the worst reimbursement rate of all plan types. The fee schedule is not negotiable and is typically posted by the local Medicaid carrier.

Most physicians feel an obligation to care for those who are in need. A few feel strongly enough about this obligation that they join a federally qualified community health center or other program and focus full-time on the underserved. Most physicians, however, can designate only a certain portion of their practice to Medicaid patients while remaining financially viable.

In our experience, the challenge of serving Medicaid patients includes the following issues:

- Relatively poor reimbursement makes it difficult for practices to pay the bills, including payroll. Accepting too many Medicaid patients can cripple a practice financially.
- Medicaid patients may have a variety of life challenges associated with or in addition to their illnesses and may require more time and education.
- Medicaid patients may have transportation challenges, and "no-show" statistics tend to be higher in some practices.
- It may be difficult for primary care physicians to refer Medicaid patients to some specialists in a community.

At the same time, serving Medicaid patients has the following benefits:

- Medicaid patients include not just the chronically poor but also those who are underemployed, students with small families, and those who are just down on their luck. Many will ultimately move from the Medicaid rolls to improved circumstances and insurance coverage.
- Providing primary care access to Medicaid patients helps them to deal with health issues before they become emergent and end up in the emergency room (or worse).
- Medicaid patients may have friends who are not on the Medicaid rolls and, like any satisfied patient, will refer their friends to their doctor.
- Medicaid reimbursement beats no reimbursement at all—but not by much. Hence, the need to control the percentage of a practice (particularly a new practice) that is dedicated to the underserved.
- Specialists who take Medicaid patients from referring physicians will also likely receive well-insured patients from those same physicians.
- Some areas with high Medicaid participation denote rural or underserved medical areas. Practicing in those areas may also offer additional financial incentives, including higher reimbursement or possibly medical school debt forgiveness.

Most states have a variety of Medicaid options. Some programs are set up to mimic a traditional managed care plan and, therefore, require primary care physicians to "manage" or coordinate both primary medical care and specialty or hospital services. The plan may even offer a small capitated fee (a monthly stipend for each Medicaid patient), in addition to the reimbursement for services rendered, to compensate the physician for the coordination of care required. Some states offer plans for both adults and children, and others offer programs only covering children.

Most states contract with a private insurance carrier to manage their Medicaid programs. The credentialing process will vary depending on that particular carrier, but the process is usually similar to other credentialing activities. Completing the Medicaid credentialing process involves four steps, and you will find they are very similar to the credentialing process for Medicare:

1. **Complete the Enrollment Forms:** The CMS website offers great resources to identify what types of Medicaid programs are offered in the region where you wish to practice medicine. By examining the plans and their purpose, you will be better able to decide which programs best fit your particular practice. Once you have made that decision, contact the state Medicaid carrier to obtain the appropriate application forms and then carefully complete those forms. When enrolling in

the Medicaid program for the first time, you will likely be completing multiple forms. These may include individual provider applications, a group application (if you are forming a group practice), an electronic funds transfer agreement, and an assignment of benefits form. Be careful to read the carrier's instructions and to complete all the necessary forms. In most cases, the same information required for completion of the Medicare application will suffice for Medicaid programs.

Most Medicaid forms also request a Medicare provider number. If you have not received your Medicare provider number when applying for participation in Medicaid, simply write "applied for" in the Medicaid application. Some carriers will not process the Medicare and Medicaid applications simultaneously, so we recommend completing and submitting the Medicaid application and then following up when the Medicare provider number is received.

If you will be using an outside billing agency or a practice management company, that information is also typically requested at the time of enrollment. If you have not made final arrangements at the time of application, you can submit a change request once your provider enrollment packets are processed.

As with Medicare, Medicaid carriers can take up to 90 days to process an application for enrollment, so the credentialing process should be started well in advance of the anticipated practice opening.

2. **Review Enrollment Forms:** As with your Medicare application, it is important that you carefully review the application to ensure that all necessary signatures and documents are obtained in all of the requested locations. Failure to do so will delay processing and any reimbursement for services provided.

3. **Send or Deliver the Application:** Again, we recommend making a complete copy of the application and attachments for use in following up with the carrier. If you are using the mail, make sure that signature verification is required. If you are hand delivering the package, we recommend that you type a small delivery acknowledgement for signature by the person (often a receptionist) to whom you hand the application. Either method identifies the date, the location, and the person who received your application package.

4. **Follow Up:** Once again, follow up with the carrier about every three weeks until you receive your provider number to ensure that progress is being made and to forestall any delays in application processing because of inadequate information. Remember the name of the person who is processing your application, and call that person back each time to follow up. Also remember that you will get further with honey than with vinegar. Be polite and respectful, but persistent, in your communication. Within 90 days, you will receive written notice of your new provider number and group billing number (if applicable). Retain these notices for your records.

Remember that once you have decided to be a participating provider in a Medicaid program, you cannot discriminate against Medicaid patients or selectively accept those patients who qualify for the program.

Credentialing with Other Carriers

Contracting with private (nongovernment) insurance carriers is vital to the success of most medical practices. Whether you are a primary care physician or a specialist, a member of a group practice or a solo practitioner, you should pay close attention to this business process. This section will focus on the credentialing aspects of the contracting process. Later in this chapter, we will discuss contract analysis.

Private insurance carriers go by a number of different names that are sometimes descriptive of their programs and sometimes not so descriptive. Terms like health maintenance organization (HMO), preferred provider organization (PPO), managed care organization (MCO), discounted fee-for-service (FFS), indemnity plan, and others will be heard as you explore the alternatives in your community. Your initial focus should be on investigating the major carriers that service a particular market area. Ask local hospital executives or local physicians to identify the major insurance players.

The following steps for credentialing with private insurance payers are the same basic steps used to complete the credentialing process for government payers. You will likely repeat them several times as you consider participating with various private plans.

1. **Selecting the Plans:** Some communities are saturated with a large number of private carriers. Others are dominated by a few. Regardless of the circumstances in your particular community and your specialty or practice setting, you will likely want to participate with the dominant private carriers in the market. As a primary care provider, this philosophy will ensure that you are accessible to large numbers of patients who can select you from their approved panel of providers. As a specialist, you will want to participate in the same payer plans as your referring physicians; otherwise, they will be forced to refer their patients elsewhere. If that "elsewhere" is your competitor, who offers better access and provides equivalent service, you risk losing a referring physician.

   Once you have targeted the private payers of interest, it is important to request their contract and application forms. Some physicians sign payer agreements and complete applications without paying much attention to the complex terms and conditions always contained in those documents. We always emphasize the importance of physicians becoming familiar with payer contract terminology and with the terms and conditions common to most payer agreements. In addition, a qualified attorney can be expensive but can save you thousands of dollars in financial losses if contract terms are inappropriate. Some medical staff relationships offer the opportunity for physicians to join an Independent Practice Association or a Physician Hospital Organization, in which physicians can combine their resources to review and negotiate payer agreements. Regardless of the process, a thorough contract review is critical before commencing the payer's credentialing process. (Again, contract review will be discussed later in this chapter.)

   The potential variety of private carriers in a particular community increases the complexity of the contracting and credentialing process. In planning the new practice start-up, you should be mindful of the potential time involved and start the process well before you see the first patient. Again, six months is not too early to commence gathering and evaluating information about plans and to request applications and contracts.

2. **Complete the Enrollment Forms:** Many states have adopted a standardized credentialing form that most private carriers will accept. The form can usually be obtained from the state's Insurance Commissioner's office. In addition to the standardized application, many of the national payers also participate in the Universal Credentialing Data Source, which is an online credentialing application database supported by the Council for Affordable Quality Healthcare (CAQH). This service is free of charge to the provider but requires a registration process

before you can build your credentialing profile. Utilizing the online database can expedite the process, because multiple payers can access the same information. You can usually complete many of the application pages once and then copy them for use with multiple payers, significantly reducing your preparation time, because only the pages requiring signatures must be originals. (*Hint:* Make sure you indicate at the top of each application the name of the payer to whom you are submitting the package.) Please note that even if you use the CAQH database, you will still need to contact the local payer to start the process. That local payer will typically send you a one- or two-page document formally requesting your authorization for them to retrieve your data.

When requesting the provider enrollment applications, be sure to ask what the approval process entails, including how long the process usually takes and when the provider review board meetings are held. Such information will help you to prioritize your preparation and speed the processing of your applications. If you are practicing in a group setting, be sure to clarify whether you need to complete any additional forms to link your application to that of the group practice.

Remember that most payers have provider enrollment information on their websites. When you request an enrollment packet, be sure to ask for the contact name and number of the local area representative. We recommend meeting and establishing a relationship with that representative early in the process.

3. **Review the Enrollment Forms:** The same careful review of completed forms is recommended for each of potentially several applications. A little time and effort up front dramatically reduces potential rework on the back end.

4. **Send or Deliver the Application Forms:** As usual, make a copy of the entire application package for each carrier, and carefully label that package to prevent confusion, especially if you are using the standard forms. Mail or deliver the package, and request a delivery signature, similar to the applications for government programs. Be aware of the regularly scheduled provider review panels for each of the payers, and deliver the package in time to allow internal review before the meeting occurs. Your local representative can assist you in timing your applications properly.

5. **Follow Up:** Expedite the review process shortly after submitting your application to ensure that no additional information is necessary, and then follow up periodically with your representative to check on the status of your application.

Credentialing Laboratory Services

There are both clinical and business considerations for providing laboratory testing within your medical practice. Clinical considerations include accuracy, reliability, and timeliness of results. Business considerations include patient convenience, capital costs, operating costs (including staff), and regulatory compliance. Laboratory services used to be potentially lucrative for group practices, but today's increased costs and lower reimbursements have dramatically reduced that potential. Usually, only those practices with large laboratory volumes can justify, on the basis of financial return, anything but the simplest of laboratory tests. The availability of sophisticated laboratory service vendors (local, regional, or national) and the convenience of rapid electronic feedback for physicians further reduce the need to provide those services within the practice. Often, outside laboratory vendors will staff a draw station even in small group practices at no cost to the physicians, providing the level of service expected by the patient and required by the clinicians. These arrangements are usually transparent to the patient, who appreciates the convenience of not having to go elsewhere for basic laboratory services.

Deciding what specific laboratory services to provide within your practice and specialty is beyond the scope of this text. Checking with other physicians in your specialty and community will help you to establish the scope of services normally expected by local patients and referring physicians.

Regardless of the scope of services that you ultimately provide, all laboratory services are regulated by the CMS through the Clinical Laboratory Improvement Amendments (CLIA). From simple urinalysis to complex chemistry tests, all laboratory services fall under this regulation. The CLIA was established to provide quality standards that would help ensure the accuracy, reliability, and timeliness of test results. According to the Medicare website, "CLIA requires all entities that perform even one test, including waived test on . . . 'materials derived from the human body for the purpose of providing information for the diagnosis, prevention or treatment of any disease or impairment of, or the assessment of the health of, human beings' to meet certain Federal requirements."[1] The regulation requires that you obtain a certificate identifying the level of complexity at which your office will be permitted to perform laboratory testing.

Five levels of certification are available:

1. Certificate of Waiver
2. Certificate of Provider-Performed Microscopy
3. Certificate of Registration
4. Certificate of Compliance
5. Certificate of Accreditation

The most commonly requested levels are the Certificate of Waiver and the Certificate of Provider-Performed Microscopy.

The process for pursuing CLIA certification is as follows:

- **Determine Your Scope of Services:** Again, we recommend starting with the local community standard for your specialty. Identify those services that are routinely provided within the offices of established physicians or, if you are the sole physician in your specialty, check with others in your geographic region. Once this information is available, you can consider those tests that you want to perform versus those that you will outsource. (A list of laboratory tests can be found on the U.S. Food and Drug Administration website [http://www.fda.gov/cdrh/clia].) Once you have identified the tests that you want to perform within the practice, consider the following questions about each of them:
  - What will be the reimbursed revenues associated with the test?
  - What will be the equipment costs associated with the test?
    - Original purchase or lease
    - Calibration, maintenance, and repairs
    - Cost of upgrades
  - What will be the cost of reagents and other supplies?
  - What level of training will be required to competently provide the test?
  - What will be the human resource costs associated with providing the test?

---

[1]http://www.cms.hhs.gov/CLIA/06_How_to_Apply_for_a_CLIA_Certificate,_Including_Foreign_Laboratories.asp#TopOfPage

- Technician
- Interpretation
- Clinical oversight

- What test volumes can be expected from your practice now and in the future? (It may be appropriate to outsource for a period of time to determine actual volumes.)

Many vendors will provide revenue and expense estimates associated with their equipment. It is always wise to do your own analysis, however, because their information is potentially biased to sell.

After you have considered the revenues, costs, and other intangibles (e.g., patient convenience) associated with each test, finalize the list of laboratory services that you will provide within your practice.

- **Determine the Level of CLIA Certification:** Based on the tests listed on the U.S. Food and Drug Administration website (http://www.fda.gov/cdrh/clia), determine the level of CLIA certification that you will need to pursue. It is also prudent to check the state requirements. Most states follow the federal guidelines, but there may be some differences in your area. Remember, the most complex test that you will offer is the test that will determine your CLIA certification level.

Keep a watchful eye over the financial impact of laboratory services on your start-up costs. Laboratory testing is one area in which the costs will add up quickly. If you decide to invest in nonwaived testing, you will need to become familiar with the minimum compliance requirements.

Certificate of Compliance laboratory testing brings with it additional levels of cost not related directly to the testing equipment and supplies. These additional costs include, but are not limited to, higher certification fees, more stringent proficiency testing requirements, certain levels of routine quality controls, outside quality-assurance measures, laboratory director requirements, staff certification requirements and others.

- **Complete the Certification Application:** Complete form CMS 116, which is the CLIA Certification Application. If you are part of a group practice, complete the application in the name of the business. If you are a sole practitioner, use your own name or the name of your business entity. Be sure to identify any additional state application requirements by contacting your local state health department. You can obtain state agency contact information on the CMS CLIA website (http://www.cms.hhs.gov/CLIA/). We recommend that you always contact the state agency before submitting the application to verify the local process and requirements.

- **You Know the Drill:** At this point in the chapter, we probably don't need to remind you about the importance of double-checking the completed application for accuracy, sending or delivering the application with signature verification of receipt, or following up until written approval has been received.

You will receive written notification of your CLIA certification number via a fee remittance coupon. This coupon will indicate the certification fee along with the compliance or validation fee (if applicable). Once the fee is paid, you will receive the formal CLIA certification for either waived or provider-performed microscopy certificates. If you have applied for nonwaived certification, you will first receive a certificate of registration, which will apply until your practice has passed the survey inspection.

PAYER CONTRACTING CONSIDERATIONS

As we have discussed, identifying and successfully contracting with the major payers is critical to your bottom line. Understanding the contracting process and protecting yourself from bad deals is just as critical as adding that payer to your panel of insurance companies. Naturally, payers will write contracts that protect their own interests (including the interests of their shareholders). You must protect your own interests. Protecting your interests can include one or more of the following tenets:

- **Always Use a Professional To Review Contract Terms, Conditions, and Language:** Someone who is familiar with the contracting process, contract terms, and contract language will be in the best position to help you protect yourself.

- **Look for Opportunities To Contract as Part of a Larger Group or Network:** It is much more difficult for insurance carriers to ignore larger groups or networks of providers. It is often safer to negotiate as part of a group, because many eyes will be looking at the same deal and the cost of professional fees can be shared. Independent Provider Associations, Physician Hospital Organizations, or other large groups may provide an opportunity to "level the playing field" in contract negotiations. Be aware that you can violate the law as you negotiate jointly with others, particularly if you are the only game in town. Again, legal counsel will be able to ascertain the appropriateness of the contracting mechanism, and most established Independent Practice Associations and Physician Hospital Organizations have already passed legal muster.

- **Don't Be Rushed:** There are very few emergencies on the business side of medical practice. Make sure you take the time to be thorough. A fast deal, with a lot of pressure, is usually not a good deal.

- **Be Engaged in the Process:** As mentioned before, you have trained to be a clinical expert. Fortunately—or otherwise—you are also in business, even as an employee. Learn the basics of payer contracts and negotiations, and you will be better off. While consulting experts, learn from them for both current and future reference.

In the following paragraphs, we will share some questions and resources that you should consider regarding payer contracting. In addition to common contracting questions found in this document, the American Medical Association provides a comprehensive contracting evaluation tool and a sample of a model managed care contract. Your state medical association may also provide payer contracting information. We strongly recommend you consult those resources as well.

As a first step, you should review a few key areas of the potential relationship before making the decision to participate. We certainly recognize the ultimate importance of the contract, and that the review of that document is crucial. A few issues that every practitioner should consider, however, will not appear in specific contract language. For example, you should consider how "physician friendly" or "patient friendly" the managed care organization is. Pay special attention to the following areas, because these affect both the provider and the office staff:

- The payer's business/financial stability
- The patient base represented
- The payer's staff support
- The payer's electronic capabilities and support
- The administrative requirements of the plan

The best way to pursue this analysis is by answering as many of the questions that follow as possible.

As mentioned earlier, understanding the patient population you are likely to serve is an important first step in the payer contracting process. Even a superficial analysis of the market will provide you with some key insights regarding the type of insurance plans that will be prominent in your area. If you are located in an aging community, you are likely to see a number of Medicare and Medicaid patients. If you are located in a community with a number of large employers and high per capita income, you are likely to see a variety of managed care plans. We also mentioned the value of consulting with the local hospital and with your peers to determine the key payers in your area. Once the key payers have been identified, you can check their websites and contact the payers directly to find answers to several important questions. Making contact with the local payer representative is usually a great way to start. You can gather a variety of data about the payer's relative position in the market, their targeted employers by size or industry type, and who they count as providers, by asking the following questions:

1. How many members does the plan currently cover in my immediate market?
2. How many members does the plan cover in other markets, and where are those markets?
3. Does the company have a marketing plan for my area, and if so, what is it?
4. What other physicians and hospitals in this area participate in my plan?
   a. You may be able to obtain some information from the plan's website under the participating providers. If not, ask for a copy of the provider listing.
   b. Ask how frequently the provider panel is updated to make certain you have the most current information.

Once you gather information about the patient population being served, you should consider the payer's financial solvency. Over the past decade, several payers have become insolvent or have been forced to sell as a result of poor financial performance. Either scenario poses a risk to you as the provider. If a plan fails, you will be left with little or no reimbursement for services you have already provided. If a plan is sold, the new owner may push for lower reimbursement rates or less favorable contract terms. It is prudent, therefore, to look at the financial health of the payer organization with which you are planning to do business. Getting answers to the following questions will help:

1. What has been the recent financial position of the company (profit or loss)?
   a. You may also be able to look up the historical financial performance information of several plans on the state's Commissioner of Insurance website.
   b. In some cases, you may even wish to request a copy of the audited financial statements for review.
2. Does the payer "rent" the network out to other insurance companies, or is it owned by another company?
3. How long has this plan been in existence?
   a. Newer plans may not be as well organized and can pose delays in reimbursement for you and in treatment authorizations for the patients.

Once a business deal is consummated, you and your staff will need to deal with the payer's operations during the term of the agreement. Before contracting, you will want to know the payer's history as a business partner. How responsive is the payer to participating providers? A few simple questions posed to plan representatives as well as to peers in the area can inform your decision. Consider the following questions:

1. Will I have a dedicated representative who will work closely with my office and assist my staff in areas needed?
2. How often will the representative come to my office?
3. How easily can I access my representative should a question arise or should I need support?
   a. Be certain to inquire with your peers or the local medical society about the accessibility of the local plan representatives.
4. Will I receive a product manual that gives clear instructions and resource information for me and my staff?
5. May I review a copy of this manual before contracting?

Another important factor in a successful partnership with a payer is the payer's electronic technology and support. As a result of the Health Insurance Portability and Accountability Act regulations, most payers accept electronic claims submissions; however, payers can do much more to facilitate a provider's practice operations. For example, electronic verification of patient benefits is a common and extremely valuable service to providers and their patients. This service may be provided by the carrier via secure access online, the payer's website, or a credit card swipe terminal. (Benefit verification should be available via a telephone access at minimum, but the most efficient and effective method for your front office staff is online capability.) Some payers will require your office to submit verification requests in advance, but the larger payers usually have real time online capability. Ask if any costs are associated with verification of benefits requests. Some clearinghouses charge as much as forty cents per request. This is a small price to pay to ensure reimbursement, but negotiations often include free data verification.

Another component of electronic support is the common electronic remittance advice (ERA) and direct deposit. With the right practice management system, both can be a boon to your practice in terms of efficiency and timeliness of reimbursement. If not implemented correctly and monitored constantly, however, they can also create huge accounting problems in a hurry. Using ERA, clean claims can be paid as rapidly as 14 days with money in the bank as soon as the claim is approved. Whether or not you choose to use the full electronic capabilities of the payer, the following questions will help you to identify their capabilities:

1. Does the payer offer electronic funds transfer (direct deposit)?
2. Does the payer offer an ERA, and if so, how is it retrieved?
3. Does the payer offer online benefit verification systems?
4. What other options are available to support the benefit verification process?
5. Can referrals or preauthorizations be obtained electronically via a secure website?

Every payer contract will require certain behaviors (administrative responsibilities) from you and your staff. Two key administrative responsibilities are verification of benefits covered and preauthorization for additional ancillary, specialty, and hospital services. In addition to these key items, you will want to understand your risk management and other responsibilities. The following questions can help to clarify your responsibilities and can be posed to your payer representative:

1. How will my staff verify coverage of benefits for a plan member, and what information will be shared following the request?
2. What information is required to obtain a referral or an authorization for a patient? Will it be obtained by online request, phone, fax, or mail?

3. Who is responsible to notify the patient of the referral request, and how will they be notified?

4. Is there a specified list of services requiring prior approval, and what services will my medical judgment justify without additional approvals?

5. What is the appeals process for a denial of authorization? Is there an Independent Review Organization process available to both patients and providers?

6. Are there certain types and amounts of liability insurance coverage required for participation in your program?

7. Will I be required to participate in a quality assurance or utilization review committee?

8. Is there a certain expectation by the payer for call coverage within my practice?

These twenty-five questions are only a sample of the considerations regarding participation with a payer. After conducting this initial analysis and requesting the contract document, you and your expert counsel will want to consider the following key contract provisions:

- **Compensation:** The compensation provisions of the payer contract should include detailed information about how you will be reimbursed for the services you render to participating members. The compensation section will help your billing staff to identify proper claims payment and your management team to plan your cash flow and develop financial strategies. A variety of compensation arrangements are available, including specifically contracted fee schedules for your services; discounts from your normal fees; usual, customary, and reasonable charges for the local market; capitation or other withholds; or some other resource-based relative value scale calculations. Understanding the values and the methodology used for calculating your reimbursement will be critical to ensure that the payer is using current rates and that you can monitor the accuracy of payments. Additional provisions relating to compensation include:
  - *Payment Policies:* How payment will be made.
  - *Utilization Policies:* Limits on services that can be provided and referrals that can be made.
  - *Noncovered Services:* Services that will not be covered by the payer.
  - *Carve-Outs:* Certain services not included in a particular plan (e.g., mental health services).
  - *Timely Filing:* Sets the time limit for the provider to make a claim based on the date of service.
  - *Timely Payment:* The payer's commitment to pay without penalty; check local and state laws governing timely payment and interest provisions.
  - *Hold Harmless Clauses:* Commitments from both parties to hold each other harmless in case of an untoward event and to cooperate in legal defense.
  - *Retroactive Denials:* The payer's ability to retroactively deny a claim.
- **Administrative Requirements:** Administrative requirements clarify how you will be expected to manage your plan members' care. Performance standards and mechanisms for member eligibility verification, referral processing, and prior authorization procedures should all be clearly addressed in the contract terms. (You can often look to your state medical society to determine if any specific state laws relate to administrative requirements.) The contract should also clearly document your appeals process.

- **Term and Termination:** Two key areas to consider during the contract review are the contract term (length of the contract) and the termination clause. Often, payer contracts specify a one-year term with an automatic renewal provision requiring notice if either party wishes to renegotiate terms. This type of clause saves you and the payer both time and energy if the contract is working for both parties, including your reimbursement. If not managed properly, however, you could experience the same reimbursement rates for years, despite inflation. Make sure that notice clauses are the same for you and the payer.

  You will also want to make sure that the contract clearly describes the circumstances under which the agreement can be terminated and the implications of termination by you or the carrier. Make sure these termination clauses are fair to both parties, not just to the carrier.

- *Other General Provisions:* There are a variety of general provisions that you will want to discuss with your experienced counsel. These include:
  - Dispute resolution and arbitration (make sure you understand which state laws govern the contract)
  - Assignment clauses
  - Required physician availability
  - Ability to close the practice to new plan patients
  - Practice schedule expectations
  - After-hours call coverage
  - Medical records copying (the carrier should pay for copying medical records for utilization review)

It would be impossible to anticipate the variety of contracts and terms you might encounter, but a final hint about successful contracting remains. Make sure that you receive and carefully review all contract exhibits, appendices, and other documents referenced in the agreement before signing (e.g., provider manuals). Also, make sure that you understand which of the payer's products or plans are covered under the agreement.

CHAPTER SUMMARY

A number of helpful resources are available to assist you in your credentialing process; for many carriers, this includes provider representatives. The CMS website is a great place to start the process. Your local medical society may also have helpful resources to guide your efforts, as will an experienced office manager. Among the best resources we have found is the Texas Medical Association website (http://www.texmed.org).

CHAPTER *Five*

TECHNOLOGY NEEDS ANALYSIS

Four key filters should drive all of your business decisions and processes in medical practice:[1]

1. Does the decision or process maintain or enhance clinical quality?
2. Does the decision or process maintain or enhance service quality?
3. Does the decision or process maintain or enhance productivity, particularly physician productivity?
4. Does the decision or process maintain or enhance practice financial viability?

If a decision cannot pass all four filters, you should modify it or even abandon it altogether.

Nowhere are these four filters more critical than in the selection of technology to support your medical practice. We live in a world of constantly changing technology that affects every facet of our lives at home, at work, and at play. If mastered, technology can serve to enhance everything we do; if not, technology can create performance challenges at lightning speed. Consequently, we must take great care in the selection, installation, training, and support of our technology systems.

A few fundamental tenets should drive technology selection:

- Technology is *relatively cheap* when compared with the costs of labor. Ensuring that people have the right technology to accomplish their work in an efficient and effective manner is paramount.
- Technology is *constantly changing*. The technology you select will likely be obsolete within months rather than years. Consequently, technology selection should include the ability to expand, upgrade, or replace at a reasonable cost.
- Your practice *requirements* should drive technology selection. Determine your needs and requirements before shopping for technology solutions. Armed with this information, you have a better likelihood of selecting tools that meet your needs, as opposed to what the salesperson wants you to buy. Buying too much capability ("bells and whistles") that you will never use can be as detrimental as not selecting enough capability. Prepare a written list of your requirements that you can give each vendor, and ask them how their product addresses your requirements.

---

[1]Cohn, Kenneth, and Douglas Hough, eds. *The Business of Healthcare, Volume 1—Practice Management.* Westport, CT: Praeger, 2007, p. 43.

- *Reliability* is paramount. The all-encompassing benefits of technology can bring our world to a halt when the power goes out or the technology fails. Purchasing systems that have a reliable performance record should be a critical part of any decision process. Devices that manage power (surge protector, battery backup) to protect and properly power down sensitive equipment and software should also be a consideration.

- *Customization* and *flexibility* are important. Consider whether your technology tools can be adjusted to your practice's workflow, terminology, business practices, and regulatory requirements—or will you need to change your practices to conform to the technology? Technology should be a tool that assists you, not one that causes you more work.

- *Service* is as important as the sale—perhaps more so. When technology breaks, it is critical to have responsive and capable service to return the system to full operating capacity both quickly and efficiently.

- The more reliant we become on our technology, the more critical the issue of *security* becomes. Equipment redundancy and backups for data and software are critical in a world of intended and unintended disruptions. Protecting data is increasingly critical to keep sensitive medical and demographic information from falling into the wrong hands—including a disgruntled employee.

Within the context of our four decision filters and our fundamental tenets, let us turn to a discussion of the basic technology you will need to practice efficiently and effectively.

COMMUNICATION TOOLS

The most important part of your business will be communicating with your customer. Your most common connection to your customer will be your telephone system. These systems do not need to be overly complicated or expensive, but you will need to spend enough money to get a system that is both reliable and user-friendly (even you need to be able to understand and manage calls). The system must be able to grow with your practice, upgrade as technology changes, and be locally serviced.

Office telephone systems are not like the telephones you have in your home. Office systems handle multiple incoming and outgoing phone calls, fax machines, voice mail, and other specialized services, which means you will pay more for the equipment. Modern office telephone systems are, in reality, sophisticated computers. The most expensive systems connect to the office PCs, and the computer mouse controls phone calls, transfers, and voice mail. Not every office needs the latest innovation, however, or even voice mail, which can double the price of a system. Understanding the needs of your practice (or a similar practice) before you begin searching for telephone equipment will facilitate a selection based on practice needs rather than "a good deal."

The process of selecting your voice system should include a review of several alternatives. Arrange to have demonstrations of different systems by different vendors, preferably with your office manager or an experienced medical practice advisor involved in the process. Share some basic parameters with each vendor in advance, and examine their solutions. These parameters should include estimates of your ultimate practice size, phone call volume, number of staff members, desired capabilities, and even your price range. Compare pricing, system capabilities, warranties, and vendor service capabilities with your office requirements. Prices for systems sold by the same vendor can vary widely. Economical systems can be priced as low as $3,000 to $5,000 without voice mail. Expensive systems can easily cost $20,000 or more, but an investment in the right system will facilitate quality care and caring, promote enhanced productivity, and support financial viability through improved service. Do not skimp on technology. Some vendors will provide a trade-in allowance when you outgrow your system, so look for a vendor that has a large enough range of products to meet your future growth.

New Versus Used

Occasionally, you might find a vendor with a used system, or you might even find a system that is being peddled on the Internet. Be very careful about purchasing older systems, especially from a potentially unreliable source. You may get what you pay for—very little! Vendors who are trying to sell a used system are typically willing to provide some warranty (usually one year), but make sure that your practice situation does not become a round peg forced into a square hole (at any price). Your best bet with a used system is to stick with a very reliable local vendor that has an impeccable service record and sees you as a long-term customer. Otherwise, as with any older computer, you will run into problems with obsolescence. Finding repair parts or replacement handsets can be tricky for systems older than five years, and vendor support becomes increasingly challenging and expensive as systems age. On the other hand, most new systems will be modularized, so you can add upgrades, such as voice mail or Voice over Internet Protocol (VoIP) as needed.

Ease of Use

If you cannot learn how to use the system in just a few minutes, do not buy it. Your receptionists and others will need to have an easy-to-understand system that can quickly and easily move calls to the correct locations. Few things are more frustrating for your patients and your referring physicians than misrouted calls or being abandoned on eternal hold. Vendor promises of extensive training will not make up for a poorly designed or poorly installed system.

Service After the Sale

Service after the sale can be difficult to assess unless you have the opportunity to talk with vendor references. As you narrow down your list of potential systems, ask to speak with other offices that use the same system. Most offices will be happy to share their experience with the system and the service. Some newer systems can be serviced remotely over the telephone lines, with upgrades and program changes being made from the vendor's office. This usually means quicker service for you, because problems can be addressed immediately. If a vendor hesitates when you ask him about the ease of servicing the system, move to the next vendor.

(By the way, do not forget to place your telephone book ads before the next telephone book is published. You may need to have your information to the phone book publisher six months in advance of the next release, so do not delay!)

Automated Attendants

Automated attendant options are available for many telephone systems today. They are efficient and effective if one is not intimidated by technology, if the selections are kept to a minimum, and if the caller is quickly given an option to reach a human. Otherwise, automated attendants can be frustrating—and even insulting. Although busy offices sometimes need the help of an automated attendant, many customers prefer to speak with a person who can acknowledge and then competently deal with or transfer their call to the right location. Customer-oriented offices will use a personal response to incoming callers unless and until call volume forces them to use an automated alternative. Then, they use automation with great care. We recommend having a separate line for referring physicians that is always answered by a human.

Voice Mail

Voice mail is another wonderful yet irritating innovation. Directing a caller to voice mail is a great alternative if a customer is trying to leave a nonurgent message in the midst of his or her own busy schedule. From the practice perspective, using voice mail properly can be an efficient way to handle telephone calls and messages. If not handled properly, however, it can be a customer service nightmare. If you add voice mail to your phone system, consider implementing policies that require you and your staff to return all phone messages promptly to reduce patient frustration and repeated calls about the same issue from anxious customers. Remember, voice mail can add to or detract from your reputation—it's your choice.

Automated Call-Back Systems

Some telephone systems work with your practice management system to automatically telephone patients and remind them of upcoming appointments, to let them know that a prescription has been called in, or to remind the patient to make a follow-up appointment. This option is an excellent time saver for your practice, because it can reduce "no-show" appointments and increase the productivity of your staff.

Office Sound System

Many offices install sound systems to broadcast music throughout the clinic. Most are simple systems with speakers in the ceilings and an amplifier located in a cabinet, usually with a CD player attached to it. The sound system serves several purposes. Sound systems help to cover sensitive conversations, can help soothe nervous patients (with the right selection of music, of course), and can contribute to a professional ambiance. (Larger clinics may add a paging system for paging employees, although it is preferred to use private paging from one phone handset and workstation to another.)

INFORMATION SYSTEMS

In addition to your telephone system, other information systems and equipment will make or break your business. For our discussion, a "system" includes the methodology or process, any software to support that process, and any equipment or hardware to house the process and/or software. From a business perspective, three main information systems drive every practice:

- A practice management system
- A medical records system
- An accounts receivable management system

All three of these systems are increasingly integrated and increasingly automated. (They are often integrated with the telephone system, as discussed earlier.) When possible, it can be better to purchase a single package that has two or more of these systems already combined or integrated. Getting systems from different vendors to "talk" to one another (share information between them) can be very challenging and costly. If systems are designed to work together and share common data, or at least easily send information back and forth, it will be easier on your staff (they will enter data only once), the data will be more accurate (you will not make mistakes by entering data twice), and it will be less expensive to purchase and maintain.

Practice Management Systems

Automated practice management systems support patient scheduling, demographic data collection, benefit verification, and point-of-service collections. They also support the accounts receivable management process, including coding, insurance billing, patient statements, and collection activities. A practice management EMR system also provides management information and analysis, including payer mix data, productivity statistics, and patient referral tracking. Increasingly, practice management systems either include or integrate with an automated patient health record.

Deciding whether to process insurance claims and statements within your practice or to hire a billing company affects your practice management system options. For those who choose to process their own bills and statements, many software packages appear to perform all of the major functions necessary for medical practice success, so deciding among the options can be difficult. In addition, most communities have outside billing companies that will provide you with access to their practice management system as part of a contract to process (for a fee) your insurance claims outside the practice setting. Regardless of the option you choose—and both options can work very well—we encourage you to think long term in your selection of a practice management option. You may not immediately need all the bells and whistles provided by many software packages, but as your practice grows, as the industry evolves, and as regulations change, you will need to select a system that can be flexible. Remember the fundamental tenets, and do not skimp on your practice management system.

Those selling practice management systems have varying levels of knowledge and experience. Our recommendation is to know what you need and want your practice management system to do before you ever contact a vendor. Most practice management systems provide the following common modules and capabilities (not an exhaustive list):

- Patient Scheduling Module should include:
  - An appointment scheduler that allows for multiple appointment types, locations, provider types
  - A master appointment template for each provider
  - The ability to perform mini-registration for new patients
  - Financial class (payer) identification
  - The ability to view and edit patient insurance information
  - The ability to search by multiple patient identifiers
  - The ability to identify potential copayments
  - Alert message features for outstanding balances, bad debts, or recurring no-show appointments
  - Integration with the patient demographic database
  - Integration with an electronic medical record (EMR)
- Patient Registration Module should include the ability to:

- Capture all pertinent patient demographic data, including employer information or guarantor information (if different)
- Input detailed insurance information to the tertiary level (up to three payers per patient)
- Verify benefits and deductibles at or before the time of registration
- Store images of the insurance card and other important information
- Report on any patient demographic data set
- Generate a fee ticket at the time of registration
- Support point-of-service collection efforts
- Billing/Accounts Receivable Module should include:
  - Point-of-service charge and payment posting
  - Batch posting to provide audit trails and balancing features
  - Denial management tracking abilities
  - Electronic claims submission
  - Claims error notifications (claims scrubbers or rules engines)
  - Electronic remittance advice posting
  - Line-item payment and adjustment posting
  - Monthly patient statement processing
  - Extensive report generation
  - Functions to address all Health Information Portability and Accountability Act (HIPAA) and billing regulatory guidelines
  - Aging of accounts based on date of service
  - Capitation payer analysis reports
  - Managed care contracting analysis and tracking
- Collections Module should include:
  - The ability to set up payment arrangements
  - A work-list format based on "tickler" systems established by the office
  - The ability to generate custom collection letters, payment receipts notices, and notices of failure to adhere to financial agreements
  - The capability to store account notes
  - Insurance rebilling capabilities
  - Small balance write-off functions
  - Extensive reporting capabilities based on flags, assigned collector, payments, and so on
- Reporting Modules should include:
  - General reporting abilities for current month and year-to-date performance
  - Edit reports for claims tracking
  - The ability to monitor transaction volumes, types, and payer contracts
  - The ability to sort data by doctor, site, location, date of service, Current Procedural Terminology (CPT) codes, financial class, payer group, specific patient demographics, and so on
  - Productivity reports available by relative value units, service units, code groups, and in summary formats
  - Audit reports available on demand in all areas of the system

Other modules can be added for items such as real-time benefit verification, insurance card scanning, occupational medicine billing, case management (referral) tracking, a report writer, managed care contract analysis, site of service differential billing (also known as UB92 billing), financial accounting modules, and EMRs. Many of these modules may be included in the base package.

Anticipated practice volume, ultimate number of physicians and other providers in the practice, number of support staff, and specialty-specific nuances are also key considerations in selecting a practice management system.

When selecting software, some practices overlook the importance of the reporting features found in a practice management system. The reporting function is critical to help identify the reasons for your successes and your failures. Most vendors will indicate that their product comes with all the "standard" reports and that additional reporting features are not necessary, but expect that you will need more than just the "standard" reports. Have each vendor provide a copy of the reports generated by their software packages, and make sure these reports meet your needs. You should also ask how difficult and costly is it to get a custom report generated. It is highly recommended that you select a system with an "ad hoc" report capability so that you can quickly create your own reports to address the new questions that will inevitably surface over time.

One final note: Software packages operate on a variety of hardware and software platforms. For example, some are Microsoft Windows–based programs. Others may be UNIX based or IBM AS400 systems. Still others may even be Web-based programs. The operating system may contribute to the ultimate cost of the system, to its user-friendliness, and to its manageability. Make sure that the system you select runs on a mainstream operating platform rather than a unique operating system. Otherwise, the costs of future maintenance may be significant.

Given the critical nature of a practice management software decision, we recommend seeking the assistance of an independent practice consultant before making this significant investment. Pay the consultant a fee, and make sure that he or she does not have an arrangement with any of the software vendors or options under consideration.

Medical Records Systems

You are already well aware of the clinical value of a medical record. You have been trained to create a progress note that documents such factors as the patient's chief compliant, his or her vital signs, the results of your physical examination, your diagnosis, and your treatment plan. Your medical record will also contain a medication list, recent diagnoses, results of diagnostic tests, forms completed by the patient, correspondence from specialists to whom you refer the patient over time, your correspondence regarding the patient, and notes from your clinical assistant. A patient's medical history will likely provide the baseline against which you will compare his or her current circumstances. These clinical factors protect the patient and allow you and your team to practice quality medicine.

Your medical record also supports the billing process. Some residency training programs do a better job than others in training physicians to code and document for billing purposes. Procedure and diagnosis coding must be supported by adequate documentation as evidence that the services were actually provided to the patient. Over the years, we have encountered a few physicians who overcode relative to the documentation they provide, placing themselves and their organizations in legal peril. In our experience, however, many physicians actually undercode and underdocument relative to the level of service they actually provide. Some physicians indicate that they are just too busy to document fully for billing and, therefore, find it easier to downcode.

Most solo and small group practices (and many large medical practices) still use a paper medical chart. Progress notes are frequently dictated, transcribed, and added, after physician review and approval, to the chart along with other paper reports, letters, and so on. Most practices have a medical records clerk (or assign the task to someone) who builds charts, pulls charts, files notes and reports, and files the charts. Most importantly, in practices of any size, staff members are also assigned (formally or by default) to find lost charts—meaning charts that have not yet made their way back to the chart room before being requested again.

In recent years, the concept of creating a standard electronic medical record (EMR— or EHR, electronic health record) has hit the public policy arena. The President of the United States and the U.S. Congress have proposed plans and articulated visions of an EMR for every citizen in the country that can be shared or exchanged with a variety of clinicians and authorized users under strict security and privacy protections. The benefits of an EMR are potentially significant for an individual practice and/or a community; however, the barriers to the success of such a vision are myriad.

According to the Centers for Disease Control and Prevention National Center for Health Statistics, use of a full or partial (part paper, part electronic) EMR among office-based physicians grew from slightly more than eighteen percent in 2001 to nearly twenty-four percent by 2005. As one might suspect, physicians practicing in larger groups were more likely than those in solo practice to use an EMR. Still, the trend in applying technology to the challenge of medical records is apparent.[2]

Early versions of the EMR provided electronic charting. The leading EMR systems today have the following capabilities:[3]

1. Electronic charting
2. Drug interactions
3. Registry function (needed for quality reporting and pay-for-performance contracts)
4. Orders for prescriptions (eRx)
5. Electronic orders for tests
6. Computerized test results
7. Computerized physician notes
8. Clinical Decision Support
9. Patient Portal

These capabilities point to several obvious benefits of an EMR. A properly implemented system can virtually eliminate much of the paperwork, storage cost, and chart hunting found in many practices. Clear and complete information can be shared with partners and with those physicians to whom the patient might be referred (assuming they have the same electronic capabilities), improving coordination of care and reducing the potential for medical errors. Importantly, clinical data are more readily available and usable in an electronic format. When combined with the patient demographic data also contained in most every system, this clinical information becomes a powerful tool to encourage preventive screening, to improve management of chronic conditions, and to demonstrate the quality of a physician's practice of medicine.

---

[2]Burt, Catharine W., Esther Hing, and David Woodwell. "Electronic Medical Record Use by Office-Based Physicians; United States, 2005." National Center for Health Statistics Health E-Stats, pp. 1–2 (http:// www.cdc.gov/nchs/products/pubs/pubd/hestats/electronic/electronic.htm, retrieved February 21, 2008).

[3] Cambridge Management Group (Kenneth Cohn, Joseph Scherger, and David Schlaifer), "Engaging Physicians to Adopt and Use Electronic Health Records," audio conference conducted May 13, 2008.

The EMR does have some downsides. The most obvious is cost. Systems are still prohibitively expensive for solo or small group practices. (Most inexpensive systems are early generations with limited capability; this is an area where you definitely get what you pay for.) The interface between various billing systems, which contain much of the demographic data, and various EMR software packages is still evolving. The costs of ongoing database management and maintenance can be significant, whether the physician is technically oriented and does the work himself or not. For established practices, the transition from paper to even a partial EMR can take as long as four to six months, during which time productivity falls. In our experience, this time can be decreased with proper levels of training, and productivity does return to or even exceed pre-EMR levels after the transition time.

In all likelihood, you and your patients will benefit from an EMR during your career. Like most technology solutions, the costs will drop over time, and the standards and resulting interfaces will be established, making the EMR more commercially viable. Until then, we encourage solo or small groups to maintain a quality paper system.

Accounts Receivable Management System

For years, we have told our clients that the most important thing they can do to ensure the success of a medical practice is to provide high quality care and caring to their patients. The second most important thing is to "get paid" for the first!

A properly selected and implemented practice management system will facilitate the revenue cycle, which in its simplest terms is the process of "getting paid." A simple revenue cycle consists of the following steps:

1. Capture/verify demographic data
2. Verify payer coverage and benefits
3. Collect copayments
4. Coding and documentation
5. Charge entry
6. Point-of-service payment collections
7. Claims scrubber
8. Primary insurance claim processing
9. Primary insurance payment posting and contractual write-offs
10. Secondary insurance claim processing (if applicable)
11. Secondary insurance payment posting and contractual write-offs
12. Denial management and outstanding claims research and re-filing
13. Statement process (patient due balances)
14. Private payment posting
15. Credit balance resolution
16. Precollections activities for nonpayment
17. Professional collections for nonpayment
18. Patient dismissal for nonpayment
19. Bad debt write-offs

As you can see, receivables management (or revenue cycle management), even at its simplest, is quite a process and requires careful monitoring to maintain a constant flow of cash coming into the practice to pay your bills and to pay you.

Today, physicians have several technology options available when managing the revenue cycle. You can choose to purchase your own billing software and equipment and have your support staff members manage the entire revenue cycle (at least steps 1–15 as well as 16 and 18). You can select a billing company and delegate many of the revenue cycle management steps to them. You can also select an Application Service Provider (ASP) that will, at a minimum, provide the application software and hardware necessary to file insurance claims and patient statements for a fee. Some ASPs may process claims as well. We can point to successful practices using all three approaches. Regardless of the alternative you select, the key to success is *management* of the process. You will want to remain actively involved in monitoring the revenue cycle to ensure that you are contributing properly (through effective coding and documentation) and that your support team and billing vendor (if applicable) are meeting their obligations as well. Again, technology can help you effectively oversee the process through appropriate and timely performance reporting.

A few advantages and disadvantages of each receivables management alternative are identified below

CONTROLLING THE ENTIRE PROCESS	
Advantages	**Disadvantages**
Total control over every aspect of the revenue cycle process.	Challenge and cost of hiring, training, and maintaining competent staff members.
Research can occur close to the medical record.	Significant capital investment.
Ability to run reports at will.	Cost of system and database maintenance.
Feedback on denial management can be immediate, potentially reducing future errors.	

USING A BILLING AGENCY	
Advantages	**Disadvantages**
The billing agency hires and trains their own staff.	Performance reporting usually occurs less frequently.
A successful billing agency manages its own performance.	Practice staff members may feel less commitment to the billing process and to maintaining an effective revenue cycle.
Usually requires a minimum investment of capital.	Loss of process control.
Most agencies are local, providing potential access to senior executives for face-to-face accountability meetings.	Potential restrictions for reporting capabilities, based on the vendor's software.
Most vendors are paid as a percentage of monies collected, so they are not paid unless you are paid.	
The billing company likely files many more claims each week than your practice will ever file. The associated experience is a great potential resource, particularly for exceptions.	

Using an ASP	
Advantages	**Disadvantages**
Low capital investment.	May be located outside your area or state.
Process large numbers of claims and develop decision rules based on that learning.	If you contract with a large processor, they will not likely focus on your practice as much as a local vendor with few clients will.
Usually offers top-quality equipment and constantly upgrades software.	

The Medical Group Management Association (MGMA) provides an excellent questionnaire to help physicians select an external billing company or ASP. The questionnaire is available at the MGMA website (http://www.mgma.com).

TECHNOLOGY HARDWARE NEEDS

Computer Hardware

The computer hardware required for your office will be determined by the approach you take to manage your revenue cycle (practice-based or outside vendor), on your practice management system, and on your EMR system (if applicable). Some practice management programs are web-based (e.g., athenaNet®), and other systems will reside in your office only (e.g., ArcSYS' Red Planet EMR). Regardless of the system you select, a few general rules apply to a hardware purchase. Look for:

- Hardware reliability
- Performance speed
- Plenty of hard-drive storage capacity
- Reliable information technology (IT) support with great response time

When working through your needs analysis, remember that technology changes about every 18 months, at a minimum—and sometimes even faster. Therefore, growth options, long-term technical support, and equipment obsolescence should be included in your thought process.

Computer Networks

Even as a solo practitioner, you will have multiple computers in your office. Each computer will likely be connected to the Internet. In addition, they will likely need to connect to one another, creating an internal network, or "intranet." There are two common approaches to connect personal computers (PCs) in an office setting. They can be connected through a central "server," or they can be connected to each other directly in a peer-to-peer network. Each of these approaches will be discussed next.

A dedicated server system diagram looks much like a wagon wheel, with a server "hub" and PC and printer "spokes" attached to it. Your EMR and practice management system will reside on the server, and every PC in the clinic can access the common software and databases through data cables or a wireless signal. (If you run a wireless network, remember to change the default password on the wireless router and enable the highest level of security; otherwise, people outside of your network could use your Internet connection and possibly access your data.) Data cables, or "hard-wired" systems, will generally be a little faster than current wireless technology, but not significantly so. Servers for small networks tend to run several thousand dollars, but they have the power and speed to accommodate many user requests simultaneously and share resources (e.g., printers, Internet connection, file storage, and practice management software). Many servers can fit under a desk, although larger systems will usually end up in a "computer closet," where the noise and heat given off by the machine will not be distracting. (Chapter Three includes an option to co-locate the network server in the telephone closet. Be sure to provide air conditioning in this space, because the heat generated can damage the equipment.)

Running a server network involves a few important challenges. A network server is complex and requires a higher level of expertise to maintain compared with individual PCs. You should plan to replace your server completely about every five years. You may also find that a hardware upgrade will be required at some point during the five-year life of the unit. In addition, dedicated servers require unique software to run properly. Do not forget to include software to protect against viruses and cyber-intruders when budgeting for the cost of the server. You will need to renew annual licenses for software, such as the server operating system, client "seats" (the number of users connected to the network), anti-virus, anti-spam and firewall (Internet-blocking). Do not be surprised to find that annual licenses (for software updates and maintenance fees) may be as much as $2,000 (or more) per program. Server software is much more expensive than PC software.

As mentioned, another common networking approach for small offices is a peer-to-peer network, in which several computers are connected via cables or a wireless signal. One of the PCs acts as both a computer workstation and a server (and must always remain ON for the other computers to communicate with one another). This approach is less technically complex and less expensive, but sophisticated programs may not work on a peer-to-peer network. For example, an EMR may not work without a dedicated server, or it may work but response times would likely be very slow, because a PC is not specifically designed to address demand from programs that require a lot of overhead (computer processing power) or from many users. Remember, the software is very different for a PC versus a true server. If your goal is to have an EMR in the next few years, it may be less expensive to set the system up with a dedicated server at the outset. Make sure your IT consultant knows what your future plans are, and have your consultant make a recommendation based on your timeline.

Another variation to a dedicated network is to have your software "hosted" at an Active Server Page (ASP). The software runs on the ASP's network, and your staff accesses the program(s) over a secure Internet connection. Review the ASP considerations listed on the following page.

Computer Workstations

Your staff members will need a workstation (PC) at their desk or work location. Several staff members may share a computer, there may be one workstation per staff member, or you may have additional workstations in high-use areas. There are several options for workstations:

- **PC:** This can be either a desktop or laptop. Each PC requires numerous software packages, including operating system software, protection software (anti-virus, anti-spam), e-mail, word processing, and more. These software packages require a certain level of expertise and interest to configure and maintain them on a regular basis (including applying periodic software upgrades).
- **Thin Client:** This is a smaller device that has no "brains." It is a small component that connects to a keyboard and a monitor, but all the processing (work) is done at

ASP CONSIDERATIONS	
ASP Advantages	**ASP Disadvantages**
Capital expenditures are lower; hardware and software are "rented" from the ASP.	You don't own the hardware and have a monthly fee, which over the life of the contract may exceed the purchase price of hardware.
Expertise is provided to maintain and configure hardware and software.	You work through a Service Desk instead of a dedicated IT person.
	Performance is usually a bit slower than with an in-house server.
An ASP allows redundancy and disaster recovery—if your network goes down, all work stops until a local IT person can get spare parts or make repairs. The ASP is responsible for "hot spares" and 24/7 support	If the ASP or Internet service goes down, you cannot access the software. May need to have paper version of critical components
An ASP can provide a dedicated Internet connection, which is monitored for service performance	An ASP need a faster Internet connection, which may cost more than you would otherwise purchase.

the server. There are no software updates or maintenance with a thin client, so not only is the purchase cost much less than a PC (under $200), there are no software licenses to buy and it costs basically nothing to maintain. Once it is set up, it works.

We recommend purchasing workstations (either PCs or thin clients) with the help of your IT consultant. Many IT companies get preferred pricing from such companies as Dell or Toshiba because of the large volume of purchases they make. In addition, some IT professionals prefer to build the desktop machines for you, which may save you money and will get you exactly what you need without paying for add-ons you may not really want.

Desktop monitors have made significant strides in recent years. This has resulted in a better-quality product at lower prices. As you look to purchase monitors, consider the space they will occupy. A reception desk or nurse's station that does not have much space will benefit from a flat-screen monitor. Although less expensive, traditional CRT monitors take up much more space. Also, make sure the monitor quality is sufficient for employees who will spend many hours staring at the screen (a monitor with more "dots per inch" [dpi] means better resolution and is easier on the eyes). A billing specialist will be more productive if her eyes do not hurt by noon every day.

Other Technology Needs

You should also consider other hardware needs within your office, including printers, copy machines, fax machines, scanners, credit card machines/benefit verification systems, and shredders.

Printers

Printers are an absolute necessity within your practice. Thankfully, the costs of printers have fallen significantly during recent years while the capabilities per dollar spent have increased. You may network several staff PCs to the same printer, but you may want to allocate specific printers to specific functions, especially those requiring preprinted forms. For example, depending on your system, you will either:

- Use preprinted forms for items such as superbills and insurance billing forms, and thus need dedicated printers stocked with those forms.
- Print superbills and insurance forms on plain paper, along with the completed information at the same time; dedicated printers are not needed in this scenario.

If you use an IT professional to purchase your PCs, inquire about packages bundling a printer with your computer purchase. In addition, you may consider a multifunction printer/scanner/copier/fax machine for start-up, which can be used as one of several printers when your practice expands and needs more equipment.

When making a decision about a printer, consider the following questions:

- Who will be using it?
    - Multiple people—a network printer
    - Single person—office manager (HR information)
    - Dedicated printer—specific use (e.g., superbills)
- Is the printer network compatible?
- What will be the volume of printing?
    - Laser printers handle a higher volume than do inkjet printers.
- How fast does it print?
    - Pages per minute (ppm) will vary greatly.
- Do I need color printing, or will black ink be sufficient?
- Do I need double-sided printing (duplex)?
- What kind of paper can be used?
    - Bond, heavy stock, labels, multipart forms.
- What size of paper can be used?
    - Letter, legal, envelopes, postcards
- How much space does it take on a desk (footprint)?
- What is the average cost per page based on the machine purchase, maintenance costs, supply costs (ink and toner cartridges), and life expectancy?
    - Is there a maintenance plan?
    - What are my practice management and EMR system requirements in terms of preprinted forms?

Copy Machines

In addition to printers, a medical practice will typically require one or more copy machines. You will likely want a copier at the front desk for copying insurance cards and receipts for patients. You will not want your receptionist leaving his workstation several times each day to make copies, so a small machine is worth the cost. Your main office copier, however, will likely need to be a bit sturdier. When you start looking into midsize copy machines, you will find an abundance of options. Among the many features to consider for the main office copy machine is an automatic document feeder. This option is a huge time saver for your staff. Another useful feature of some copiers is the capacity to serve multiple purposes, such as a basic copier, a network printer, a fax machine, and a document scanner. The higher-end models even provide document storage for those repetitive forms and print jobs. Copiers can range from $1,000 for small machines to more than $10,000 for medium-duty copiers that will meet the needs of most small medical practices. The make and model of the copier are not as important as the warranty and the service contract. Most companies offer lease options that can help with the initial financial strain of large-dollar purchases, but beware of the lease payment options. They often end up costing far more than an initial outlay and service arrangements would have cost. Obtaining competitive bids from several resources is a wise investment of your time and can prove very beneficial in negotiating a purchase price. It is also important to remember that ink or toner cartridges are relatively expensive, and that cost should be considered in the purchasing decision.

Some questions to consider when looking into copiers and their functionality are:

- What types of copying and printing functions will it most often perform?
- Is an automated collate function important?
- What do the toner cartridges cost?
- What are the service contract options and minimum usage requirements?
- What is the average cost per page based on the machine costs, maintenance costs, and supply costs?
- What are my practice management and EMR system requirements?
- Is the machine network compatible?
- Will a multipurpose machine result in inefficient operations within the office (e.g., will staff stand around waiting for access or larger printed reports)?
- What basic job functions will dictate the need for a dedicated printer/copier?
- How will the physical layout of the office affect the location of the main copy machine?

Fax Machines

While some copy machines offer fax capabilities, volume and use should be considered when deciding whether to purchase a dedicated fax machine for the office. Some medical specialties will have greater incoming and outgoing fax volume than others and require a reliable and dedicated fax machine (and the accompanying telephone line/cost). Primary care specialties tend to have high fax volumes because of prescription refills/requests, home health orders, referral requests, benefit verification requests, and ancillary test results. Like printers, fax machines require ink or toner cartridges that may be relatively expensive despite a low upfront machine cost. Some practices reduce fax costs by dedicating a fax machine to incoming faxes only and buying a less expensive model to use for the fewer outgoing faxes. Your server may also be able to conveniently accept and send faxes as well.

Another option is to use an electronic fax service. For a low monthly fee (which gives you a certain number of pages a month, with a per-page charge after the limit is reached), you are given a local or toll-free fax number for incoming and outgoing faxes. When you receive an incoming fax, you access the service via the Internet and print the fax. To send a fax, you scan the document, attach the file, and send it to the fax number you designate. An electronic fax service is a viable option, particularly in the early days of your practice when you do not know the volume of faxes or if you want to be able to access incoming faxes from your home or other location.

Scanners

Scanners are used to make a digital copy of a piece of paper (e.g., the patient's insurance card). The resulting file can be attached to a patient's EMR, e-mailed to a referring physician, or even submitted to a payer. Scanners have many features, including making digital images in black and white or in color; have varying levels of resolution; come with an optional document feeder (highly recommended); can reduce/enlarge the image; and more. A scanner can be a stand-alone piece of equipment, may be part of a multifunction printer, or could be found on a network copier. Be sure to include scanning capability in at least one of your pieces of equipment.

Credit Card Machines/Benefit Verification

Another hardware component you will need to consider in setting up your new business is a credit card swipe machine. Accepting credit cards is an excellent way to ensure payment at the time of service as well as to collect outstanding balances. You can purchase traditional desktop credit card machines through your financial institution or other independent credit card companies. You can also surf the Web and find resources in your area for credit card machine arrangements. Beware of the fine print in agreements discussing the various service charges. Some less reputable companies offer a low upfront machine cost but charge exorbitant transaction fees. Desktop machines can range between five-hundred and several thousand dollars.

As technology has improved, there are now Internet-based credit card systems, which are much more cost-effective than the traditional machines. Newer swipe machines can actually save you money, because many financial institutions are beginning to charge more for transactions that are keyed manually. The automated card swipe component costs about $150, and the software for the Internet-based service should be free or offered at a minimal charge. Before setting up this service, be sure to check with your practice management system vendor. Many practice management systems now come with credit card transaction capabilities already built-in.

An additional consideration is a machine that provides multiple functionalities by conducting benefit verifications as well as credit card payments. Your practice management system should do this via the Internet, a clearinghouse, or direct integration with the carrier. Some carriers, however, such as Medicaid, still require a physical card swipe machine. Your local Medicaid carrier can tell you if a card swipe machine is required and can suggest companies that provide such equipment.

Shredders

The HIPAA requires a cross-cut shredder to ensure privacy protection. We find shredders priced as low as $50, but some models can run several hundred dollars. As a new business, you will not likely need a heavy-duty machine. You might purchase a smaller machine that can later be moved to your personal office and replaced by a higher-capacity machine as the practice grows. You can also look to outsource your shredding to a licensed document destruction company. For a minimum fee, document destruction companies will typically provide a locked container that is picked up according to a regular schedule. The contents are then either shredded at the site or are taken off-site for shredding. One final consideration is to check into what the companies do with the shredded material. Some companies are in the business of recycling the material, which of course is the most environmentally friendly way.

CHAPTER SUMMARY

Technology will be a significant portion of your start-up budget. As we noted earlier, however, we encourage you not to skimp on technology. Your most expensive resource for ongoing operations will be your human resources. Properly selected and properly implemented technology solutions will enhance your productivity and the productivity of your support staff. Technology will also improve the quality of your care and caring by helping you properly address the needs, wants, and priorities of your patient customers, their families, and your referral sources. Consequently, technology will ultimately facilitate the success and financial viability of your practice.

CHAPTER Six

STAFFING AND HUMAN RESOURCES

REGULATIONS TO REMEMBER

In 1938, the U.S. Congress passed a landmark labor law called the Fair Labor Standards Act (FLSA). This law resulted in sweeping changes to the way that employers dealt with their employees. The law was so comprehensive and so important that it has survived the test of time. You might ask, "What does this have to do with me?" The answer is "Plenty!" As a business owner, you are required to know, understand, and follow the labor laws that apply to your medical business. Not knowing these rules could result in fines, civil action, and in the most severe cases, criminal prosecution. This section will review the basics of federal labor laws. (Importantly, many states will have additional laws or rules, and you need to be aware of those as well.) Your attorney or state workforce services office can help you to understand what additional requirements you have in your state. Remember, the federal law sets a minimum standard; state laws can only add to the federal requirements.

Hours Worked

Many business owners have fallen into the trap of forcing their employees to work extra hours without pay. The basic rule is simple: For every hour your "hourly" employees work for you, you must pay an hour's wage. After working forty hours in a week, you MUST pay one and one-half times their regular wage for every hour worked over forty hours. Even if the overtime is not authorized, you must pay it if the employee worked it. Hours worked can be rounded to the nearest quarter hour. Hourly employees in a medical office usually include nurses, medical assistants, receptionists, file clerks, and other similar employees. All are eligible for, and should be paid for, overtime hours worked. Be sure to check your state regulations for what constitutes "overtime." Some states have additional situations that trigger overtime (e.g., any hours worked over eight hours in a single day).

Some employees are "exempt" from the overtime pay rule because of their "professional" status. These employees will likely include physicians, physician assistants, nurse practitioners, and potentially, your office manager. These employees are paid a set salary or some combination of salary and bonus as opposed to an hourly wage. They cannot have their pay reduced for hours not worked in a week. There are certain rules that define exempt employees, so make sure that yours pass the test. The U.S. Department of Labor Fact Sheet 17A, which defines the rules for exemption, is found at http://www.dol.gov/esa/regs/compliance/whd/fairpay/fs17a_overview.htm.

What about your office manager? You must be able to show that he or she is truly a "professional" employee. An exempt office manager should (1) have a supervisory role over at least two other full-time employees, (2) either have the ability to hire and fire or have significant influence in the decision to hire or fire, (3) have the authority to discipline employees, and (4) have the authority to make some decisions regarding how the business is managed.

Some small business owners have attempted to define every employee as "exempt" in an attempt to avoid paying overtime. This tactic is a violation of the law and can result in fines and payment of back wages if an employee complains to the authorities.

Other small business owners have attempted to use compensatory time instead of paying overtime to hourly employees. The use of compensatory time, or "comp time," as it is often called, in lieu of paying overtime is a violation of the FLSA rules governing overtime—even if comp time is preferred by the employee. Comp time is accrued time off (extra paid days or hours off) that is taken at a time other than during the workweek or pay period when the overtime occurred. Forcing or allowing your employees to exchange overtime for comp time can eventually lead to a complaint to the state and a fine. A strict policy against compensatory time is your safest route.

The FLSA also sets a minimum wage. Some states have set a higher minimum wage with which you must comply. You will probably find that you have to pay much more than the minimum wage to attract and retain good employees.

Short rest periods for snacks or coffee must be counted as hours worked. Bona fide meal breaks (e.g., lunch) are not work time. An employee who is required to attend a lecture, meeting, or training program during or outside regular work hours should also be paid for the time spent in these required activities. If the attendance is voluntary and outside regular work hours, no pay is required.

Recordkeeping

The law requires you to keep accurate records of all hours worked by every person you employ. This requirement is not as onerous as it sounds. Good timekeeping software that will track and record hours worked by your staff can be purchased for less than $100 and loaded on a personal computer. More complex systems using electronic time cards are also available. For a small office, however, all you really need is a basic approach. You should keep your payroll records, including time cards, for a minimum of seven years. External payroll vendors are available in most markets and can assist in the recordkeeping process for a fee if you choose to outsource your payroll.

Other Tidbits

A few other common wage and labor issues may arise in the course of running your medical practice business. Some of these issues include:

- Child labor laws generally preclude you from hiring anyone under the age of 16 years (with a few exceptions).
- You must have proof of the employee's right to work in the United States in the employee's personnel record (e.g., a copy of a Social Security card or a "green" card).
- If you terminate an employee, you must pay any wages due within 24 hours of the termination. An employee who resigns may be paid with the normal payroll cycle.
- An employee alleging a violation of the law must bring suit within two years of the violation. These legal cases are handled in an Administrative Law court.

- State laws may differ from federal law, and you also need to know local provisions.
- Many legal battles occur over the payment of overtime. Make sure your pay policies are consistent with federal and state laws by having your written policies reviewed by an attorney—and make sure you follow your written policies.
- Remember, there are exceptions to certain rules as they apply to certain industries and professions outside of the health care arena, so do not get confused with a special exception that does not apply to your business.
- For more information or answers to commonly asked questions, go to http://www.dol.gov/esa/whd/flsa.

Policy Manual Issues

Your human resource policy manual needs to reference several items to comply with the FLSA. These items include the following:

- The workweek begins at 12:01 AM Sunday until midnight the following Saturday.
- Normal hours of work are 8:00 AM to 5:00 PM Monday thru Friday (or the hours you choose to be open for business).
- The supervisor must approve all overtime in advance. Employees will be paid for all overtime worked, but failure to get advance approval, except in emergency situations, may result in discipline or termination.
- Make sure you add policies for witness duty, jury duty, funeral leave, and military leave.
- Each state may also have certain policies that should be included in your policy manual. Your attorney can advise you regarding the additional policy manual provisions applicable to your situation.

Notices

You will be required to post certain notices in your place of business regarding such things as minimum wage and Occupational Safety and Health Administration (OSHA) regulations. You will receive regular offers in the mail regarding the sale of posters to address these requirements. For about $30, you can order a laminated, full-color poster with every federal notice you need to post (and a few extras). Alternatively, you do not need to spend any money to get the regulations. You can get all of the required posters for free at http://www.dol.gov/osbp/sbrefa/poster/matrix.htm. This is an official U.S. Department of Labor "poster" page, which can provide you access to every federal poster you need to display. Below are links to the individual posters, so all you need to do is print them out:

- http://www.osha.gov/Publications/osha3165.pdf (OSHA-required poster regarding workplace safety)
- http://www.dol.gov/esa/regs/compliance/posters/pdf/eeopost.pdf (poster stating that you abide by the antidiscrimination laws)
- http://www.dol.gov/esa/regs/compliance/posters/pdf/minwageP.pdf (FLSA poster that notifies employees of their right to a minimum wage and overtime pay)
- http://www.dol.gov/esa/regs/compliance/posters/pdf/fmlaen.pdf (Family Medical Leave Act poster; applies only to employers of 50 or more employees, so you probably won't need this one right away)
- http://www.dol.gov/osbp/eppac.pdf (poster that contains a notice regarding an employee's rights to refuse a polygraph test)

These posters or notices need to be placed in a "conspicuous" location, usually the breakroom or some other nonpublic area of your practice that is frequented by staff members. Failure to post this information can result in fines, so take the time to print and post them. Again, be mindful that there may be state-specific posters that also need to be displayed. You should be able to download those from the state workforce services website.

These and other workplace regulatory requirements seem to be significant burdens, but establishing proper policies and procedures can ensure that your practice easily complies with workforce rules.

HIGHEST AND BEST USE STAFFING

In a personal service business like a medical practice, human resources (including the physician) are the most significant investment you will make. It is only through people (you and your employees) that you can organize to deliver and get paid for the medical services you provide. Managing your human resources is also important because they are the single largest expense in a medical practice. Failure to organize and properly manage your human resources will ensure the failure of your venture.

As you organize and distribute the work or tasks within your medical practice, it is important to realize that some human resources fill primary roles and that others fill secondary roles. The *primary roles* are those that interact most directly with the patient to affect his or her experience in your office. The *secondary roles* include all other job positions that support the primary roles. The three primary roles are the receptionist, the clinical assistant, and the physician (or other provider). The support staff in medical records, the cashier, the appointment scheduler, the referral desk, and even the ancillary services staff will certainly have contact with the patient, but their work will be focused on supporting the primary roles.

Highest and best use staffing simply means organizing the work of the office to ensure that the high-cost physician does what only a physician can do and delegates everything else. The clinical assistants are focused on patient care, customer service, managing the examination rooms, and managing the physician's productivity. Tasks such as referral or preauthorization calls are delegated to a secondary role—even to an extra clinical assistant, if necessary. The receptionist greets patients, gathers and verifies data, collects copayments, and monitors the reception room. Other less important (meaning nonpatient contact/management) tasks are assigned elsewhere. Balancing workloads in this way ensures improved customer service, promotes quality clinical care, increases physician productivity, and as a result, improves practice viability. Hiring adequate clerical staff to support the flow of paperwork and other secondary activities is much wiser than forcing physicians to fill out forms that they only need to sign or forcing nurses to hang on the telephone while the physician moves his or her own patients.

Ideally, a physician should lift his or her pen only to sign his name. Ideally, a clinical assistant should be at the exam room door every time it is opened by the doctor. Ideally, every customer is greeted by a receptionist with a pleasant smile within seconds of entering the practice. Only if the work of the practice is properly allocated can such ideals be achieved.

Implementing the highest and best use ideal starts with the following steps:

- List all of the functions normally found in a medical practice setting. (Developing an exhaustive list for your specialty may require the help of a consultant or other experienced office personnel.)

- Assign appropriate functions to the three primary roles.
- Assess the number of secondary staff you will need to absorb the remaining functions.
- Create an organization chart that documents the functions assigned to each position. (A sample functional organization chart is presented as Exhibit 6a.)

The functional organization chart will become your ideal organization. Granted, if you are starting a new practice, it is not prudent to hire all of your staff at once, just to watch them sit around all day with only a few patients. Receptionists may need to answer the telephone until the practice becomes busier. Clinical assistants may need to make the referrals calls while they are seeing fewer patients as the practice grows. You, the physician, may even need to fill out paperwork that in time will be completed by others and only signed by you. Do not lose sight of the proper organizational structure, however, or as the practice becomes busier, your clinical quality, service quality, productivity, and financial viability will be suboptimal.

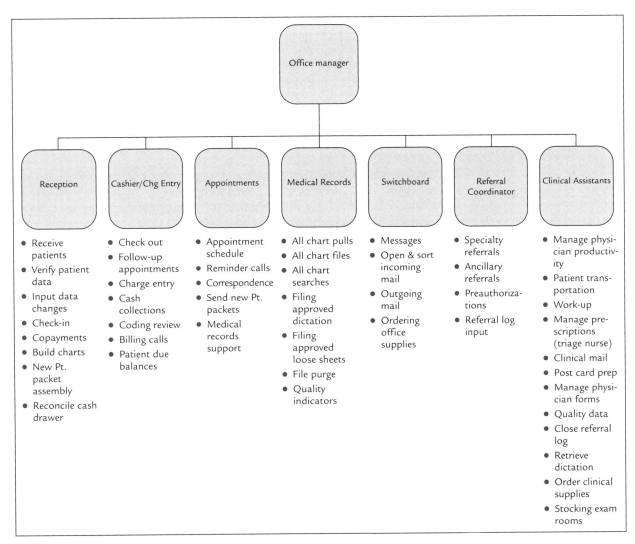

EXHIBIT 6A FUNCTIONAL ORGANIZATION CHART

Although you and your small staff will fill multiple roles during the early days of your practice, you will require job or task specialization as patient volume increases. The "Jack/Jane of all trades" is great for a small practice setting. As the volume and complexity increase, however, failure to specialize will result in poor customer service and lower productivity for all. The ideal functional organization chart will guide you as you hire additional staff to address practice growth.

Highest and best use staffing is an approach that will ensure your success even (and especially) on your busiest days. It will ensure the effective use of your most significant resource in meeting the needs, wants, and priorities of your patients/customers in a way that will promote the viability of your medical practice.

DOCUMENTING ROLES, RESPONSIBILITIES, AND REMUNERATION

Establishing Job Roles and Responsibilities

Once you have divided the job responsibilities and created a functional organization chart, the next important step is developing job or position descriptions before hiring staff. A position description defines the incumbent's role, clarifies reporting responsibility (e.g., "Who's my boss?"), documents key job requirements, and provides a basis for evaluating job performance. Position descriptions should be considered "works in process," because they will evolve as the practice grows. We recommend that each incumbent review his or her job description at least once each year to make sure that it is still reasonably current. In fact, it is often useful to review each job description in connection with a formal annual performance review.

The standard components of a job description include:

- **Title:** The job title should reflect the nature and function of the position. It may be a very general title, such as "patient service coordinator," which might include all the front-office duties in a small practice. In a larger, more complex practice, job titles might be more specific to a particular task. For example, you might divide the front-office tasks into "receptionist," "cashier," "switchboard operator," "appointments specialist," "referral coordinator," and others. An accurate job title is more important than it might seem. The title is used to advertise a position to attract job candidates with the right skills. The title can be used to identify appropriate benchmarks to help determine a competitive wage range. Titles are also important to many current and potential employees and may even be considered status symbols by some.

- **Major Job Function:** The position description should include a brief summary of the incumbent's major role. Clarifying this key job function becomes critical in positioning the incumbent on the organization chart and in identifying responsibilities, authority, and accountability for achieving the organization's objectives.

- **Reporting Relationship:** A person's supervisor, or "boss," plays a critical role in his or her success. The supervisor usually helps to define the job, hire the incumbent, train the new hire, direct the efforts of all staff members, and evaluate job performance. An accountability culture requires that everyone has a clear understanding of "Who's the boss?" Defining the reporting responsibility also helps to clarify, in the minds of others within the organization, the incumbent's authority or authorization to act.

- **Full- or Part-Time Status:** Most practices need a cadre of reliable full-time workers who provide consistency in the delivery of care over time. Part-time workers can also add value, particularly in providing occasional coverage for full-time workers on vacation or sick leave. Too many part-time workers, however, can create challenges in terms of continuity from day to day, creating frustration for both customers and their employee peers. In a medical practice, full-time status may be as little as 32 hours per week. It is important to clearly set the expected minimum hours to be worked, because this minimum will affect scheduling and employee benefit accruals.

- **Key Functions:** The functions list is the heart of the job description and usually includes the key responsibilities required to successfully fulfill the role. We always recommend the use of the term "other duties as assigned" as a final responsibility on every position description.

- **Qualifications:** Importantly, the job description should document the key responsibilities of the job as well as the education, experience, licensure requirements, skills, and abilities that are required to fulfill the role.

- **Other:** Job descriptions may also list such things as the physical effort required to perform the job (e.g., lifting requirements and amount of time standing/sitting), unusual travel requirements (e.g., a practice with regional outreach), or safety hazards affecting the position.

Exhibit 6b is a simple format that may assist you in getting started with your own position descriptions. Other good sources of information about the design and construction of job descriptions as well as the key roles found in the practice setting are also available. The Medical Group Management Association can provide excellent resources for the new manager or small practice just starting out. A simple search of the Internet will provide a wealth of resources as well.

Establishing Support Staff Compensation Ranges

Compensation management is a very important component of a successful medical practice—and one with which small practices or groups often struggle. Compensation is a very complex subject, but we will provide some basics for your consideration in getting started. The following paragraphs will discuss the objectives of compensation in a small medical practice, the importance of wage or salary ranges, and some principles of basic compensation management.

There are reams of analyses, articles, books, and opinions about the topic of compensation. In our experience, the following might be included as reasonable objectives for a compensation approach:

- To compensate people for the *time* they spend helping us operate our business;
- To compensate people for the *expertise, training, and experience* they bring to our practice;
- To compensate at a *market rate* to attract and retain good people;
- To compensate people as a reward for their *personal performance*; and
- To compensate people as a reward for the *organization's performance*.

Determining a pay range for each position is a critical first step in compensation management. A pay range will commonly have a high point, a low point, and a midpoint. The low point represents the pay rate necessary to attract a person who meets the minimum standards for the position. A candidate with documented experience or skills above the minimum required might command a wage closer to the midpoint. Offering a wage above

EXHIBIT EXHIBIT 6B
POSITION DESCRIPTION

TITLE: Receptionist—Solo Practice

REPORTS TO: Office Manager   **FLSA:** Nonexempt

PRIMARY FUNCTION/GENERAL PURPOSE OF POSITION:

To represent our physicians and staff in welcoming patients to our practice, in person and by telephone, and preparing them for their office visit through an efficient and effective registration process.

1. Candidates must possess excellent communications skills as well as compassion and a service orientation.

2. Work requires interpersonal skills necessary to function as liaison between physicians, office staff, and the patients and their family members.

3. Work requires knowledge of physician office operations, policies, procedures, and equipment.

4. Must be able to handle a fast-paced environment in a confident, professional manner. Must be self-motivated, possessing good judgment and initiative, along with the ability to prioritize and coordinate several tasks simultaneously while retaining a confident, knowledgeable, and helpful demeanor.

5. Ability to listen compassionately, demonstrating effective problem-solving and critical-thinking techniques.

ESSENTIAL JOB FUNCTIONS:

1. Welcomes patients who contact our practice by phone or in person.

2. Serves as the primary liaison for patients and the practice to ensure that patients have a positive experience while they await their visit.

3. Answers phone in a manner consistent with practice policy, triages calls, schedules patients, and enters necessary information for patient scheduling into the computer system in a timely and accurate manner.

4. Registers patients in the practice as they present for their appointments. Collects missing information, verifies insurance coverage, and collects necessary copays and/or collection balances from patients.

5. Processes fee slips as patients leave the practice. Schedules follow-up appointment and/or assists with scheduling other services for patients.

6. Pulls patient charts as needed per office policy, files information as appropriate in chart per policy, and routes charts to clinical staff as indicated in office per policy.

7. Performs all assigned duties in a manner consistent with appropriate customer service.

8. Performs other duties as assigned.

WORKING CONDITIONS:

A. General office environment.

B. Like all medical office roles, the individual performing this job may anticipate coming into contact with human blood and other potentially infectious materials. Individuals in this position are required to exercise universal precautions and, as indicated, to use personal protective equipment and devices and learn the policies regarding infection control.

APPROVALS: Date:

Office Manager_____   _____   _____

Physician _____   _____

the midpoint, even with very experienced candidates, presents a challenge, because there is limited upside potential for the employee who may be overqualified or overexperienced for the position. Such an employee may not remain with the practice for long, creating upheaval and frustration for all.

Identifying appropriate pay ranges can be challenging, but there are potential sources of help in most communities. Some states require that employers participate in a wage and salary survey every one or two years. This information is then made available to all employers in the state. State medical management associations (e.g., the Medical Group Management Association) also often conduct local or regional surveys for members and will make that information available for a small fee. In addition, a local practice consultant will be able to provide insight regarding appropriate wage ranges for support staff positions. Local information can be validated with national or regional surveys conducted by such groups as the Medical Group Management Association. You will also learn about local wages from the candidates you interview for positions in your organization. While interviewing, pay special attention to their qualifications, experience, and wage or salary history.

Once you have established pay ranges, you will likely need to visit those ranges every twelve to twenty-four months to remain attuned to changes in the market—even if you do not need to hire anyone new. We do not usually recommend cost-of-living adjustments to employee pay. Instead, we recommend cost-of-living adjustments to the pay ranges themselves to ensure they remain competitive for current or potential new employees. An employee should then move through the market-competitive wage scale based on individual performance and additional experience.

Managing compensation is a challenge for even the most savvy human resource professional. People tend to have an insatiable appetite for money. The more we make, the more we spend. Does more money motivate higher performance at work? Yes and no. The debate about money as a motivator has gone on for years. One thing is for sure—namely, we have to offer fair compensation to attract good people, and we need to continue paying fair compensation to keep good people. In general, we recommend the following simple compensation management rules to our clients:

- Hire people at or below the midpoint of any compensation range so that they have some upside over time if they continue to perform well.
- Never increase a wage or salary above the maximum level. Wait until the wage range moves to accommodate growth in the incumbent's wage. Paying employees above market rates for their skills and experience is a disservice to those who might leave (or who might want to leave) your employ but cannot find comparable compensation opportunities elsewhere.
- We recommend that you never make compensation decisions in a vacuum. Seek counsel from your office manager, accountant, or other trusted advisor to reduce the influence of your own biases and to counter undue pressure from individual employees.
- We recommend that you remain aware of wage increases being offered in the local or regional marketplace so that you can remain competitive. Increases are usually represented as a percentage of the current wage or salary and may vary by employee type. For example, you may learn that clerical staff members in the community are seeing increases of three percent this year. There may be more competition in the market for LPNs, who are seeing five-percent increases.
- Be prepared to review each employee's wage on an annual basis. This review most often occurs as part of a formal performance evaluation process.

Hiring and keeping the right employees are critical to the success of your medical practice. Employee turnover is extremely costly in terms of service disruption and the effort required to hire and train someone new. Offering the right compensation is key to attracting and retaining good people, but so is offering the right type of employee benefits. It is important to realize that the perceived value of certain employee benefits will vary by employee. Nevertheless, you will want to conduct a little research in your market area to determine the standard benefits being offered to those in other medical practices, particularly in your specialty.

Typical Employee Benefits

Health Insurance

Health insurance is usually the most expensive and most coveted employee benefit. Health insurance plans typically consist of an insurance policy offering, at a minimum, major medical coverage, but plans may extend to routine wellness and pharmaceuticals. Most practices must offer some level of health insurance to attract and retain workers. During the past few years, health insurance premiums have increased at double-digit rates, placing significant pressure on large and small businesses alike. As the costs of health insurance premiums have continued to climb, many employers have started sharing the costs of the benefit with employees. Most practices require the employee to contribute on some level to the cost of the insurance. Participation may range from ten to fifty percent for employees, which is significant relative to the wages typically paid for clerical positions in a medical practice. A multitude of product lines and package variations are available to help manage the cost of the premium (e.g., deductibles, prescription drug plans, copayments, and coinsurance). It is also important to remember that health insurance plans are typically priced based on the health of the entire group, so someone in the group with a serious condition or a major medical event will generally drive up the premium costs for all.

Health Savings Account

To address rising health insurance costs some medical groups are starting to offer a new form of health benefit coverage. Recent legislation found in the Medicare Prescription Drug Improvement Act of 2003 provided for a new type of health insurance coverage called the health savings account. A health savings account combines a high-deductible insurance policy with a tax-exempt health savings account. Both the employer and the employee can contribute to the plan, which is owned by the employee. These plans are a component of the Consumer Directed Health Plans signed into law in December 2003. The health savings account provides for tax-free savings to be used for health care expenses that rollover each year if unused and can generate interest earnings. In theory, these accounts provide an incentive for employees to manage their health care expenses wisely. Because this plan option is relatively new, it has not been widely adopted, but it may provide a significant opportunity for small employers.

Retirement Plan

Another commonly offered benefit is a retirement plan. Although not traditionally significant to the "twenty-somethings," this benefit naturally becomes more important to employees who are a little older or are concerned about the longevity of Social Security benefits. Even for small businesses, a variety of retirement plan options are available. Most are relatively simple to administer, but they vary in their setup and professional administration fees. Plans can be designed with a wide range of options: employee-only contributions, employee contributions with an employer match (up to a maximum percentage), employer-only contribution, profit sharing, or even employee-only contributions to start but with an option for employer match/profit sharing at a later date (typically when your practice has become financially viable).

Even if you start a retirement plan without employer contributions, providing a retirement plan is a significant benefit, because it gives employees a real tax savings. By allowing employees to invest with "pre-tax dollars" (retirement contributions are deducted first, then only the remainder of the salary is taxed), the net cost to invest in a retirement plan is considerably less than you think. And by providing a retirement plan for your employees, you also establish a retirement plan for yourself.

Most plans provide a variety of mutual fund options, which are chosen by the employee. Within your plan, you can determine the waiting period before an employee can participate (e.g., on Day 1 or Day 90) and determine any "vesting period" (the amount of time before the employee is entitled to keep any employer contributions), which rewards those who remain employees for a certain period of time. Your tax professional will be able to help you identify which retirement vehicle is the best option for you and your practice. There are a variety of retirement plan specialists to choose from; interview several to find one who will structure a plan to handle your start-up situation as well as provide room for growth.

Other Insurance

Life insurance and dental insurance are two insurance products provided by some employers in addition to health insurance. These insurance benefits usually are less critical to a competitive offer and are generally part of an insurance benefit package offered by an insurance vendor. A small standard life insurance option is often relatively inexpensive to provide to your employees. Some employers provide higher levels of life insurance coverage to the professional and administrative staff.

Another form of insurance that can be found in benefit packages is disability insurance. A disability insurance policy provides for continued compensation as a percentage of your usual compensation in the event you are unable to work because of a certified medical disability. Disability insurance plans can cover short-term or long-term disabilities. Short-term benefit plans are those that will begin providing compensation after a brief period of inability to work, such as six or nine weeks, and the coverage period is usually limited to a brief period of time. Long-term disability will not become effective until a longer period of time elapses after the qualifying injury, illness, or event, such as three to six months. Typically, disability benefits are made available with the premium cost borne by the employee. Special consideration should be given by the employee as to how the premium is deducted from their wages (e.g., before or after taxes). Make certain you have an insurance representative or tax professional explain how this benefit should be handled for your employees.

Paid Time Off

Paid time off (PTO) usually includes vacation time, holiday time, and sick time and likely is the most common employee benefit required to hire and retain full-time staff. Managing this benefit requires clear policies on how much time will be allowed, how it will be allocated, whether it can be carried into the following year, and whether it is paid out when an employee leaves the practice. Traditionally, practices have split time off into three buckets, or pools, for vacation, holidays, and sick leave, and these pools are treated differently.

Vacation pay is intended to help employees rest, relax, and recover from the constant pressure of work. Vacation is frequently offered only to full-time staff and is usually considered to be "earned" by the employee as additional income. Any outstanding vacation time is usually paid to the employee on his or her departure from the practice and may be governed by state regulations. For new employees, vacation time may be one or two weeks during the year. Employees with greater tenure may receive the additional benefit of more time off (e.g., three weeks annually after five years of service). Rarely, however, is time off for vacation extended beyond four weeks in a year because of the disruption that occurs as staff members take their earned time. As an inducement to use vacation time for its intended purpose, employers will often require staff to use or lose all of their vacation time each year or will allow only a few days (usually a maximum of five days) to be carried over into a new calendar or fiscal year. This "use it or lose it" approach also keeps the practice from having huge vacation liabilities for long-term employees. Some employers allow their employees to cash out up to 40 hours of vacation time each year (a nice benefit around the holidays), but because this option defeats the purpose of rest and relaxation for those accruing fewer days each year, we do not usually recommend the practice. A few hours of vacation time is usually earned during each pay period rather than offering a lump sum to employees.

Most practices recognize a standard number of holidays and pay their full-time staff for those holidays. The standard list most often includes the following six days:

- New Year's Day
- Memorial Day
- Independence Day
- Labor Day
- Thanksgiving
- Christmas

Some employers recognize other days and celebrations, but these six are the standard holidays recognized by most businesses. Holiday time is usually provided as it occurs to all full-time staff regardless of tenure, and it is not accrued or paid out when an employee leaves the practice.

Sick time or leave is perhaps the most challenging of the time-off benefits. Obviously, when employees are injured or ill, they should not be at work to "share the joy" with peers and patients alike. Most practices will permit employees to accrue up to five days of sick leave each year, and some allow two years of accumulation (10 days total). We usually recommend that small practices cap sick leave at this level because of the temptation for some employees to abuse the privilege. Taking time off for surgery or delivering a baby will quickly exhaust a bank of five sick days. We recommend that employees either use their vacation days or take the time off without pay when their sick leave is exhausted. Some organizations require employees to provide a note from their doctor when they take sick leave; others use an honor system. Sick leave is not paid out when staff members leave your employ. Pay particular attention to state regulations governing sick time in your locale.

An alternative approach to separate vacation and sick leave benefits that is gaining popularity among management teams is the PTO pool. The PTO pool combines accrued vacation and sick leave hours, and it leaves the management of that time to the employee. (Holiday pay is most often kept separate from the PTO pool.) Again, we recommend that limits be placed on the accumulation of PTO hours and that employees be required to use most of that time each year or lose it (with the exception of carrying over a few hours into a new year). Most PTO plans are set up on an accrual basis, meaning that the employee earns a few hours of time off during each pay period, and PTO time is usually paid out when an employee leaves the practice. The PTO approach eliminates some of the sick leave abuse of the past, because employees have control of the use of the time off.

There are a few other forms of PTO to consider as you establish your practice. These include time off for unforeseen events, such as bereavement, military duty, and jury duty. Bereavement leave allows employees to take PTO for making funeral arrangements and attending services for a loved one. The deceased individual usually must be an immediate family member, and the maximum number of days allowed per year is usually two or three.

Military leave is governed by the Uniformed Services Employment and Reemployment Rights Act of 1994. In addition, several states have added their own requirements to protect the rights of military personnel who are called to active duty. The federal law allows an employee who is called to active military duty to take leave without pay and, on satisfactory completion of his or her service, gives that employee the right to the same or a similar position as the one held just before the leave of absence. The law also protects the service person's eligibility for benefits and seniority.[1] Medical practices, as employers, are required to comply with the federal statute as well as applicable state statutes. You should obtain legal counsel from an attorney who is familiar with the state laws in your selected area.

According to the U.S. Department of Labor, there is no federal requirement for employers to pay employees who are called to jury duty.[2] Rather, any benefit is to be arranged between the employer and his or her employees. Some states have enacted laws governing employers whose employees are called to serve as jurors. Paying for jury duty does acknowledge the civic responsibilities of all employees and allows the employee to be kept whole for a specified period of time, such as three to five days. Employers generally require some evidence of jury service whether the employee receives pay or takes leave without pay. Some employers will compensate the employee for the amount of regular earned wages above the amount paid by the court for jury service. Others will continue paying the employee their full wage and then require that any amounts paid by the court are turned over to the employer. Check your local laws to see how jury duty is to be handled in your locale.

Uniform Allowance

Many physician practices require staff to wear uniforms in an effort to maintain a professional appearance throughout the office. Some employers will provide and pay for the first uniform. Others will purchase the uniforms and allow employees to pay for them over time through payroll deductions to soften the financial impact, which can be particularly important for new employees.

Establishing Your Employee Benefits Package

Obviously, a variety of benefit packages are available to employees in your area. To hire and retain top-notch employees, it is important to understand not only which benefits are offered but also how other physician offices share the cost of those benefits with their employees. Like compensation data, employee benefits information will likely be available through local professional organizations, your state medical society, or through input from your peers. Your certified public accountant, your attorney, or your practice management consultant may also have insights about benefits commonly offered in a local prac-

---

[1]Douglas, Bruce, and Daniel Balllintine. "Rights of Employees Requiring Military Leave: The Uniformed Services Employment and Reemployment Rights Act," December 15, 2001, p. 1. http://larkinhoffman.com.

[2]http://www.dol.gov/dol/topic/benefits-leave/juryduty.htm.

tice setting. Benefits vendors, such as insurance brokers, will be an excellent source of information regarding common cost-sharing practices in the local market.

A key question to consider in developing and implementing your benefit package is who will qualify for benefits in your organization. Many of the specifics are left up to you as the employer. The federal government does provide certain guidelines, however, particularly for employers with larger numbers of employees, so be cognizant of those regulations as your practice develops.

Perhaps the status of the employee is the best place to start in determining who will receive employee benefits and at what cost. Full-time workers generally receive a higher level of benefits than part-time workers (who often receive no benefits at all in a small practice). Exempt employees may receive certain benefits not available to nonexempt workers. Some clinics will even differentiate between the benefits offered to "professional" staff (e.g., physicians, midlevel providers, and management) and nonprofessional workers. Regulations provide for uniform and fair treatment of employees regardless of race, gender, religion, disabilities, or even health. You will certainly want to work with someone who is familiar with not only the federal regulations but also the state laws, because those may be even more restrictive or complex.

We often recommend working with a single insurance broker—ideally, one recommended by other physicians in the area—to develop and implement your benefits as a package. An insurance broker can be a tremendous source of information regarding products and local trends in your industry and should be able to provide basic information about federal and state regulations governing the products offered. Another alternative is to utilize an outside payroll company that has access to large benefit pools and can pass along the discounts associated with a larger group of employees. During the past few years, some Independent Practice Associations (IPAs) have found ways to organize a benefit package they make available to their entire membership, thus passing along the reduced per unit administration costs and large group pricing to their members.

As mentioned earlier, offering competitive compensation and benefits to your employees is essential to the survival of your practice. Naturally, there is a cost associated with those competitive offerings. In established primary care practices, the combined cost of compensation and employee benefits for nonphysician employees usually should be less than thirty percent of anticipated collections or net patient revenue (collectable dollars). In specialty practices, this ratio should be lower. Take care to be as accurate as possible in developing your practice pro forma (or budget) based on the compensation and benefits information you gather for your local area.

THE EMPLOYEE MANUAL

The employee manual is a document containing the key policies and procedures that relate to the people (human resources) employed within your practice. The employee manual documents your intent and helps to protect you as the owner of the business. It clarifies your employment policies for your office manager and your staff. A properly written employment manual can protect you from the temptation to make "special deals" with persuasive employees. It can also protect you in case of an employment grievance or litigation—if you have followed your own policies. (Your employee manual can condemn you if you don't follow your own policies!)

This policy manual usually contains your expectations as an employer regarding standards of conduct, compensation policies, employee benefits, personal appearance, personal accountability, performance appraisal and reviews, work hours, safety, and other relevant topics. Typically, a manual is provided to each employee when he or she is hired, and the new employees are required to sign a brief statement indicating they have received and reviewed the policies. Some practices place a complete employee manual in an easily accessed location and provide a condensed handbook version for employees to retain in their possession.

Many resources are available to you for creation or customization of an employee manual. Excellent resources can be found in the product listings of medical practice management associations. A very thorough resource is *How to Recruit, Motivate, and Manage a Winning Staff* by Laura Sachs Hills, which is available from Greenbranch Publishing.[3]

The Introduction

The introduction gives you an opportunity to welcome each employee and to share the mission of the practice, your vision for the future, and the values you expect your team to espouse. It also gives you the opportunity to share your practice philosophy and to describe the culture you hope to create. The introduction may also contain an organization chart showing the relationship of various positions in the practice and reporting responsibilities. If relevant in your state, it will also likely contain a definition of "at will" employment, meaning that the employer can terminate the employment relationship without cause. Finally, the introduction may indicate how the manual might be changed over time, how it will be updated, and how employees will receive notice of those changes.

Hiring and Orientation

This section of the manual includes much of the regulatory foundation for the manual. It would be wise to visit with your legal counsel regarding the proper wording and appropriate disclaimers. In today's litigious society, your legal counsel could find themselves defending you one day, so getting their input up front may ultimately save you time and money. Topics that might be found in this section would include:

- Policies regarding Equal Employment Opportunity, harassment, the Americans with Disabilities Act, proof of citizenship, and right to work
- Policies and procedures regarding your hiring process, including job postings, reference checking, employment testing, nepotism, and conflicts of interest
- Policies and procedures describing your new employee orientation process, employee training, professional licensing, and education requirements

Wage and Hour Policies

This section will be of significant interest to your employees and should be included in any employee handbook. It documents such issues as the pay period, how and when time off is earned, how wages are paid, and how time off is managed. Topics will likely include:

- Pay periods and pay frequency
- Description of potential payroll deductions, including the required federal and state tax withholdings
- Your overtime policy and the authorization process

---

[3]Hills, Laura Sachs. *How to Recruit, Motivate, and Manage a Winning Staff: A Medical Practice Guidebook.* Phoenix, MD: Greenbranch Publishing, 2004. (800) 933-3711

- Your attendance policy and punctuality requirements
- Your definition of breaks and meal periods
- Any employer-covered expenses, such as travel, mileage, and meals

Performance and Discipline Policies

In this section, one should find a detailed description of annual performance review policies, probationary policies, the steps taken in a disciplinary process, as well as performance incentives (if available). When identifying the disciplinary process, you will need to be aware of the state laws governing employee dismal. Can you fire "at will" or only "for cause"? It would be prudent to check with your legal counsel regarding the practice standard for disciplinary processes in your market. Many organizations use a three-step process that includes a verbal warning, a written warning with a probationary period, and then dismissal. Other topics that might be found in this section would include:

- Performance improvement initiatives, such as continuing education
- Pay raises, promotions, and position transfers
- Standards of conduct
- Criminal activity and drug policies
- Disciplinary process, terminations, and job abandonment
- Exit interview process

General Policies

These policies will cover a much broader scope of material; they become the catchall section for items that do not fit neatly in any other section. Some of these policies may seem obvious, but it is better to be safe than to assume that someone knows and then later deal with a legal claim. Sample topics that might be found in this section would include:

- Office hours, meeting schedules, and methods of notification
- Personnel records and employee right to privacy
- Voice mail, Internet, and e-mail policies
- Personal appearance
- Personal use of telephone, office equipment, and computers
- Medical services offered to employees
- Disclosing any potential conflicts of interest (outside employment)

Benefits

This section explains in detail each type of benefit that you will offer, as discussed earlier in this chapter. In addition, this section should include a reference to workers' compensation, unemployment compensation, and Social Security benefits available to employees.

Safety Policies

Although this section tends to be brief, it is a critical compliance section. It will briefly define the general safety requirements within your business. More specifically, it will define the required OSHA standards and reporting process in the event of an injury. You would also place in this section information regarding your smoking policy and any policies against violence.

Service Standards and Patient Relations

This section describes the service standards for all employees regardless of job description. This section becomes an important tool in laying the foundation for the customer service expectations. Topics would include:

- Telephone etiquette
- Patient relations
- Health Insurance Portability and Accountability Act (HIPAA) regulations and patient confidentiality

Job Descriptions

This section should contain samples of job descriptions within the practice. It is recommended that job skill competencies also be included to demonstrate the basic level of skills needed to perform the respective jobs. For obvious reasons, we do not recommend placing wage and salary information in the employee manual. Employees who are curious about their own wage range or the range for a position to which they might aspire should inquire about this information through the office manager.

TRAINING AND ORIENTATION

Frequently, employees are hired and placed in their positions with relatively little in the way of orientation to the organization and training in their particular position. Unfortunately, failing in this important area has several potentially significant consequences. Taking on a new job is stressful for most of us. People generally do not like to fail, nor do we like the feeling of fumbling around, of looking and feeling incompetent. Being thrown into a new position with only limited training is a source of frustration for the employee, for coworkers, and especially, for customers. In the worst cases, customers leave, relationships between coworkers are damaged, and the new employee goes out to lunch and never returns. Taking the time to think through and document (with even a simple list) an orientation process and a training process can ameliorate much of this problem. Remember, the first few days will affect the employee's long-term opinion of you as an employer and will be a key indicator of employee longevity.

Orientation is the process of acquainting the new employee with the organization and "the way we do things around here." The orientation process is an opportunity to create first impressions and to set the stage for an employee's comfort and success in his or her specific position. During the orientation process, you and your manager will want to inculcate ("to impress upon the mind") the mission of the organization, its vision, and its values. You will also want to continue to sell the benefits of being part of your practice and to confirm the new employee's decision to join your team. The orientation should include both informal and formal policies. Clarifying issues such as payroll, lunch breaks, time off, dress codes, office parties, and other particulars is critical to help the new employee feel comfortable as quickly as possible. It is also critical that performance expectations, including your views on customer service, be set. The orientation should clarify how the employee can provide feedback and ask questions within the organization—in particular, how to report concerns. Your orientation checklist will ensure that you cover all the bases, and it can become part of the employee's personnel file upon completion.

Initial training efforts should be guided by the list of specific responsibilities in the position description referenced earlier in this chapter. (This list of responsibilities may be supplemented by a list of specific tasks developed for training purposes.) Training will likely include specific skills needed to accomplish the tasks as well as knowledge to respond effectively to customers and coworkers. The training process may include assignments to vendors, such as for software training, or to coworkers. The training program should also include a specific timetable and competency testing. The manager should always be personally involved in the training process and in monitoring the progress and competence of the new employee. The tasks, assignments, timetable, and competency testing should all be included in a simple action plan that may be accomplished during a probationary period or that may extend for several months.

Putting the candidate to work as soon as possible is key to effective training. All the conceptual discussion in the world is no match for having to do the work. Even experienced new hires, however, should be monitored closely during their first few days of work in your practice. Importantly, we recommend identifying your trainees (via name badge) for patients/customers, who are more likely to be understanding if someone stumbles who is new to the position.

Dedicating time and attention to properly orienting and training your new staff members will pay large dividends in terms of longevity, customer service, and coworker satisfaction.

LET'S HIRE SOMEONE!

Now that you have been armed with a basic understanding of your responsibilities as an employer, identified how you will divide the work, sorted out compensation and benefits for your support staff, documented your human resource policies, and developed an orientation and training process, you are ready to source, screen, interview, and hire employees. Identifying and hiring great people for your new business is a significant challenge. Success in this endeavor yields significant returns. Failure can be deadly! New employees are not always what they seem to be during the interview process. Sometimes, professionally embellished resumes and well-rehearsed interviewing techniques mask a candidate's weaknesses. Checking references and soliciting feedback from former employers produces only limited results because of fears about potential litigation. No hiring process is foolproof, but a few simple steps can greatly increase your potential for success.

Sourcing candidates, screening resumes, conducting telephone screening interviews, scheduling face-to-face interviews, extending offers, allowing employees to provide adequate notice to their current employers, and allowing adequate time for orientation and training usually takes several weeks. Make certain you allow adequate time to find the right candidates. We recommend starting the sourcing process no more than three months in advance. Ideally, be prepared to conduct face-to-face interviews six weeks before opening your practice and to make offers four weeks in advance, allowing your new employees to be courteous to their current employers and give adequate notice (usually two to four weeks). This timetable, of course, depends on the job market in your area. Markets with nearly full employment may require additional time and aggressive tactics to staff your new practice. Contact the local department of labor for information on the job market trends and the potential candidate pool.

Identifying Technical Skills and Successful Behaviors

The first step in effective hiring is to identify the technical skills and the behaviors that will make employees successful in their jobs and at achieving your vision or objectives for the practice. Technical skills usually are easily identified, but successful behaviors required may not be as readily apparent. For example, if the organization's vision includes a team culture in which everyone expresses his or her opinion about everything, you might seek candidates who are less inhibited and who demonstrate a willingness to communicate verbally. Your recent development of the position descriptions, task lists, and an orientation plan should help you to identify the skills and traits you are seeking. Place these criteria or traits on a simple score sheet that you can use after each interview to rate each candidate. The score sheet helps to ensure that each candidate will be assessed against similar criteria. It can also help to reduce interviewer bias and confusion when multiple candidates are interviewed over time.

Sourcing Candidates

Sourcing candidates is the second step in the hiring process. Tapping people you know to recommend for candidates (word-of-mouth referrals) will typically provide great "internal" applicants. Such networking provides the benefit of a personal referral from someone you trust about someone they know and, presumably, also trust. If you are new to the community or if personal referrals fail to yield all the candidates you need, you will have to use less reliable, external options. People of all skill levels and experience turn to the help-wanted ads when looking for positions. Well-written ads in community newspapers can be a great source of qualified candidates for most organizations—after you wade through the majority of the resumes, which will turn out to be irrelevant. (One warning—do not put your telephone number in the ad, or you will have to deal directly with dozens of people whose skills and experience are irrelevant to the position.) Newspaper ads can be specific to a single job, or they can be display ads that identify several job opportunities in the same organization.

Private agencies and recruiters can be a great source of qualified candidates. These organizations usually screen the candidates, which eliminates a significant burden. Professional recruiters and temporary/placement agencies, however, usually charge hefty fees for their services. For nonexecutive positions, they frequently pull from the same candidate pool as your own newspaper ads. The state employment service is often a good source of entry-level candidates for those who are willing to invest in training good people. Established practices might also consider connecting with local academic programs by providing "externships," or on-the-job training. This is usually an inexpensive way to source potential new hires. Having the opportunity to see these potential employees in action during their training program gives managers and potential coworkers a great opportunity to test not only skill level but also the "fit" with your practice culture. Even if the externship involves paying the employee, the rate is usually nominal, and the potential benefits are high.

Of special note as you source candidates, it is not uncommon in small office settings to find a spouse or other relative of the physician involved in the practice. The argument frequently used for such nepotism is the vested interest of the related party in the success of the enterprise. At the same time, experienced employers know the danger in hiring someone you cannot fire. Hiring relatives places an extra burden on coworkers and on supervisors, especially if the relative is connected with someone in a management or an ownership position. Even hiring support staff members who are related can present challenges if the performance of one or the other is, or becomes, inadequate. Disciplining or terminating one related employee may cost you another—and in a small office of three or four employees, that's half your workforce! We recommend, as a best practice, avoiding nepotism.

Screening Resumes

The third step in the hiring process is screening the resumes (and often the accompanying cover letters). Initial screening involves comparing the job skills and experience in the resumes with the job requirements. This comparison will usually eliminate a good share of the unrelated resumes you will receive. Once you have narrowed the list of potential candidates, we recommend prioritizing the remaining resumes based on their levels of experience and relevant skills. Then, starting with the most skilled/experienced personnel, conduct brief telephone interviews with the following key objectives:

- **Ask:** The telephone screening interview is your first chance to begin assessing personality and behavior. We do not recommend a detailed review of the resume. Instead, we will usually initiate the conversation saying something like "I have your resume, but tell me a little about you and your interests and goals." This open-ended question gives articulate people the opportunity to "sell" themselves to you. You might also ask, "What is prompting you to look for a new job opportunity at this time?"

- **Share:** Once the candidate has spoken about himself or herself, you should share a little about your vision and objectives for the practice. This information should be brief.

- **Listen:** During your admittedly brief interaction, listen carefully to the candidate, and try to identify obvious personality traits. Think about how you feel when talking to the person. How would your customers feel talking to this person?

- **Learn:** Most candidates will not share their wage and salary history when they respond to an ad—even if that information is requested in the ad. During the telephone interview, it is critical to ask candidates to share their wage history with you by saying something like "Can you tell me what you have been paid in your last two positions?" Some will counter with a question about your salary range, which you should be prepared to share and then request, again, their salary or wage for their last two positions. If they are not interested in sharing that information, it may indicate that they have been paid beyond your range, which is not a good sign (assuming you have done your homework and set your wages properly, as discussed earlier).

- **Inquire:** It is always good to inquire as to the candidate's availability. Those who want to give their current employer notice get points for being respectful. They will probably treat you the same way.

- **Explain:** End the call by explaining your hiring process: Tell the candidates that you will be conducting several screening interviews by telephone, that you will then invite selected candidates for face-to-face interviews, and when you expect to make an employment offer to the selected candidate, and then end the call.

You might conduct several telephone interviews until you have identified two to four top candidates for a position. These candidates can then be scheduled for face-to-face interviews.

Interviewing Candidates

The fourth step in the hiring process is the face-to-face interview, but the following discussion also relates to the telephone interviews discussed above. All human beings are "blessed" with the challenge of biases, prejudices, or gut reactions to people and situations. Obviously, there are laws governing discrimination based on age, gender, race, sexual orientation, and so on. Interviewers must take extra care to avoid violating these legal/regulatory mandates with inappropriate interview questions designed to elicit information about these protected topics. We encourage you to consult with a human resource expert or legal counsel regarding these issues.

Overcoming personal biases that are not governed by law can be even more challenging. Little things like a candidate's hairstyle, tone of voice, or clothing can influence your attitude. Overcoming these biases can help to ensure that each candidate is treated fairly and objectively in the interview process. More importantly, overcoming bias can keep you from losing a top candidate who had "a bad hair day." Earlier, we discussed a criteria-based score sheet as a means to help reduce interviewer bias. In advance of your face-to-face interviews, we recommend listing a few nondirective questions (questions that do not have simple "yes" or "no" answers) to test for the skills, experience, and behaviors listed on the score sheet. Identifying your questions in advance also reduces the risk of violating the law and helps to reduce inconsistencies in the interview process.

Given the "professional" resumes and interview training some candidates receive, a major objective of the face-to-face interview is verifying information about the candidate. This can be accomplished by asking detailed, nondirective questions that cover the "who," "what," "when," "where," "why," and "how" of a candidate's experience. Using words like "describe" and "explain" are great ways to solicit more useful answers. (Verification can also occur during reference checking, which will be discussed shortly.)

The interview process may vary, but it usually includes an initial review of the candidate's experience, followed by the interviewer sharing the specifics of the job requirements and giving the candidate an opportunity to ask questions about the position and to discuss ways his or her experience might contribute to success on the job. A formal written and current job description is indispensable during the interview process. Depending on the nature and complexity of the job being considered, the interviewer may also choose to pose certain hypothetical situations and ask the candidate to respond based on his or her experience. The interviewer should prepare these scenarios in advance to ensure that they both comply with the law and are consistently applied to all candidates for the same position. Again, depending on the position, the interview should also include some basic competency testing related to the job for which the candidate has applied, such as typing, use of computer software, or demonstration of a clinical skill (e.g., taking blood pressure). Complete the interview by allowing the candidate to ask any remaining questions and by sharing your timetable for making a decision. Let them know they will receive a communication advising them one way or the other. (We usually recommend sending a respectful "rejection" letter to every candidate who took the time to participate in a face-to-face interview; this letter should thank them for their time and wish them well in their career pursuits.)

At the end of each interview, the interviewer should take several minutes to complete the score sheet. In addition to the score sheet, we recommend that the interviewer make notes about his or her gut reactions to the candidate. Sometimes, just a feeling of comfort or discomfort can contribute to a good hiring decision. Good notes are particularly important when interviewing several candidates to avoid biasing your selection toward the most recent interviewees.

After completing the interview, you will want to review the scores carefully and contact the references provided to verify previous employment and competence. As you narrow down your selection, don't hesitate to contact the candidate for a follow-up question or to request a second interview if you are unsure. Take the time necessary to make certain you have the right person for the job.

Again, in conducting both telephone interviews and face-to-face interviews, it is critically important to remember there are requirements or guidelines governing the questions you can ask before employing someone. Like other employment practices, preemployment questions are governed by federal law, and some states have additional requirements to prevent unfair practices in the employment process. Generally, your preemployment questions cannot include inquiries that would reveal the applicant's marital status, national origin, age, gender, sexual preference, children, race, color, height or weight, handicaps, religious preference, economic status, and other factors. You can generally ask for the applicant's full name, place of residence, whether they are older than 18 years (legal age for employment), whether they can submit verification of their right to work in the United States after employment, and level of education. You can also request references. You can usually ask about their job experience and other factors found on their resume. You can explain general job requirements and ask if they are able to meet those requirements. As mentioned earlier, please confer with your local legal advisor or practice consultant regarding requirements specific to your locale.

Extending Job Offers

The fifth and final step in the hiring process is to extend the job offer. We recommend that you contact the candidate to personally make that offer. Your verbal offer should be followed by a written offer detailing the highlights, including the position, wage or salary, start date, and other special considerations. It should also include a sunset clause, such as "This offer will expire on September ___, 200_," and a signature line for the candidate to accept the offer and fax a copy back to you. Such documentation will help to avoid surprises and incorrect expectations for both parties.

THE PERFORMANCE APPRAISAL PROCESS

One of the most significant responsibilities for ongoing management of a medical practice is the appraisal of employee performance. I repeat, one of the *most significant responsibilities* is performance appraisal. Unfortunately, documenting performance (good or poor), providing honest and timely feedback, and listening to employees is often an afterthought, because we become so busy addressing matters that seem to be more "urgent." Nevertheless, those organizations that consistently and effectively appraise performance can develop individuals and teams that achieve great results in terms of quality and service, yielding the financial outcomes every great practice can experience.

Documenting performance

We have found that a modified "critical incident method" of performance appraisal is a most effective method for documenting positive and negative performance and providing for timely communication with employees.[4] Simply stated, the critical incident method requires the manager or physician owner to *observe* (or gather) and *document* both positive and negative job-related incidents for each employee and to store these incidents in the employee files. Critical incidents might include a significant compliment from a physician, a peer, or a patient about a particular employee. They might also include a complaint or an error that was clearly the fault of the employee. These incidents are documented and placed in the employee's personnel file for current and future reference.

---

[4]See "Usability Body of Knowledge, Critical Incident Technique." http://www.usabilitybok.org/methods/p2052.

Communication

When an incident is documented, the manager *communicates* individually with the employee soon thereafter. The manager expresses appreciation or congratulations for a positive critical incident, which is a most powerful motivator. Alerting physicians to positive events so they can also comment to the employee magnifies the value of the feedback.

The manager also discusses openly *and* respectfully negative critical incidents and solicits factors that contributed to the poor outcome or event—including barriers to performance created by the manager or owner. In communicating the critical incident, the manager listens for training barriers, motivational barriers, barriers created by established policies, procedures, or methods, and barriers created by others within the organization. Importantly, once the barriers are identified, the manager and the employee discuss and document their plans to overcome those barriers. For simple issues, a commitment to improve or change behavior may be adequate. More complex problems and barriers may require a formal performance improvement action plan that can be monitored over time by the employee and the manager.

Formal Appraisal Process

Most organizations engage in a formal performance appraisal process on an annual basis. Employees are individually ranked using a performance appraisal tool, which facilitates a quantitative scoring of an employee's performance relative to his or her roles and responsibilities (as documented in a position description) and to other employees in the organization. Many performance appraisal "forms" are available, but we recommend a fairly simple approach using three scoring categories, as illustrated below:

Below Expectations	Meets Expectations	Exceeds Expectations
1	3	5

This simple appraisal process is applied to each of the employee's key duties, as documented in the position description. Every employee is assumed to "meet expectations" in each area unless a critical incident note was placed in the personnel file during the most recent year or current feedback justifies a higher or lower outcome in a particular area. The scores for each key duty are averaged to yield a number somewhere between 1 and 5.

This formal appraisal approach has several benefits. First, it forces management to update position descriptions at least annually to more accurately reflect the current job. Second, it promotes the documentation of critical incidents to justify a score for each key responsibility. Third, it helps to prevent "whitewash" appraisals, in which everyone is given a "5" regardless of their performance.

The steps to formal performance appraisal are fairly simple:

1. The manager reviews the employee's position description to make sure that it accurately reflects the current role. If the role has changed during the appraisal period, the manager may need to work with the employee to ensure that the description is up to date before the formal appraisal process commences.

2. The manager reviews the employee's personnel file for critical incident notes. The manager should also solicit current feedback from physicians and others affected by the employee's current performance.

3. The manager scores each key area of responsibility according to the critical incident notes and current feedback. (Remember that every employee meets expectations in every key area unless there is specific feedback to move the score higher or lower.)

4. The manager totals the scores for each key responsibility and then divides them by the number of responsibilities appraised to yield an average score, which will range between 1 and 5.

5. The manager reviews the scores with the physician/owner for approval before presenting the formal appraisal to the employee.

6. The manager meets with each employee to review the appraisal and to discuss the scores. The manager listens for feedback on the scoring and on barriers to performance.

7. The manager and the employee discuss opportunities for performance improvement, and they record objectives for the coming year.

8. The employee is provided the opportunity to share his or her response to the formal appraisal in writing.

9. The final appraisal is signed by the manager and the employee and then placed in the employee's personnel file for future reference.

The physician owner will need to conduct the formal performance appraisal for the office manager.

Merit Pay

Many practices conduct formal performance appraisals for all staff members at the same time each year. Others appraise an employee's performance on the anniversary of his or her date of hire. Both methods have their pros and cons. We recommend the first method, which creates a flurry of activity for the manager and the owner over a few weeks but allows more effective comparisons and distribution of dollars set aside for merit pay increases. We do not usually recommend "cost of living" pay adjustments for staff. An increased cost of living will, instead, be recognized in upward adjustments to the pay ranges as described earlier in this chapter. An employee who is performing well will move through the wage range over time, receiving the benefit of that pay range adjustment.

We prefer to see merit pay distributed according to formal performance appraisal scores, weighted by the employee's wage level. We recommend identifying the dollars available for pay increases over the coming year as a percentage of the current payroll and then distributing that budgeted amount according to the weighted scores. The process is simpler than it may sound. For example, an overall increase of four percent on an annual payroll of $133,120 would yield a budget of $5,324.80 in additional payroll dollars for the coming year (ignoring employer taxes). This amount might be distributed as illustrated in the example on the following page.

This model multiplies the "Current Hourly Wage" by the "Appraisal Score Average" to yield the "Wage-Weighted Score" for each employee. Each "Wage-Weighted Score" is divided by the Annual Total "Wage-Weighted Score" (203.25) to yield the "Percentage Total Weighted Wage" for each employee. The "Percentage Total Weighted Wage" multiplied by the "4% of Budget" increase allocated to the total staff yields the "Percentage Annual Budget." This number is the percentage of the budgeted annual dollars that are allocated to each employee. Dividing this number by 2,080 annual hours for a full-time employee is the amount of the employee's merit pay increase. The merit pay increase, added to the "Current Hourly Wage," yields the "New Hourly Wage." Taking the difference between the "New Hourly Wage" and the "Current Hourly Wage" and then dividing the result by the "Current Hourly Wage" yields the "Percentage Change" in the wage rate per employee.

Staff Member	Current Hourly Wage	Appraisal Score Average	Wage-Weighted Score	Percentage Total Weighted Wage	Percentage Annual Budget	New Hourly Wage	Percentage Change
Manager	$22.00	3.25	71.50	35.18%	$1,873.18	$22.90	4.09%
Clinical Asst.	$18.00	3.50	63.00	31.00%	$1,650.49	$18.79	4.41%
Receptionist	$11.00	3.00	33.00	16.24%	$ 864.54	$11.42	3.78%
Biller	$13.00	2.75	35.75	17.59%	$ 936.59	$13.45	3.46%
Annual Total	$133,120.00		203.25		$5,324.80	$138,444.80	
4% of Budget	$5,324.80						

CHAPTER SUMMARY

On occasion, we have heard frustrated managers lament that without people and computers, their organizations would operate very smoothly! There is no question that managing people can be a significant challenge. At the same time, there is no more important asset to any organization than the people who develop, promote, sell, and deliver the products and services the organization provides. Automated telephone attendants and robotic physicians may comprise medical practices of the future—hopefully, a distant future. Until then, properly hiring, training, staffing, organizing, motivating, compensating, and appraising the performance of people will be the most wonderful challenge we face as managers and physician owners of medical practices. Human resource management cannot be an afterthought. It must be our prime directive, because it is through people that we provide high-quality medical care in a caring manner. It is through the organization and efforts of people that we are productive and generate the income necessary to remain financially viable.

CHAPTER *Seven*

NEW PRACTICE PROMOTION

After you have selected a community, developed your facility, and hired your staff, it is crucial to "get the word out" about your availability to provide services. If you are a primary care provider, you will need to communicate directly with potential patients. If you are an internal medicine subspecialist, you will need to announce your availability to potential referring physicians and, depending on your specialty, directly to patients. Invasive specialists usually need to connect directly with other physicians, who will likely encounter and refer most of your cases. We refer to this "getting the word out" as *promotion*. Promotion is a subset of a much larger topic called *marketing*. The purpose of this chapter is to discuss practice promotion rather than the full scope of marketing, which includes consumer research, product development, promotion, pricing, and product or service delivery.[1]

Ideally, promotion should begin several weeks before actually seeing your first patient, and it should continue in one form or another for as long as you practice. Yes, ultimately, your primary care practice will fill up, but there is always a natural attrition caused by patients who leave town, those who pass away, those who are forced to leave by payers, and even a few who leave because they are unsatisfied. In fact, we recommend that even established family medicine, general internal medicine, and general pediatric practices maintain a new patient ratio (new patient office visits/total office visits) as high as ten percent. Specialists must also continue to promote their practices to referring physicians, although as we will see later, the tactics vary significantly from those used by primary care physicians.

The following paragraphs provide the basics of practice promotion, including:

- Your practice identity
- Direct-to-consumer promotional tactics
- Referral source promotional tactics
- Customer service as practice promotion
- Promoting your practice for life

---

[1]A more complete discussion of marketing concepts is presented in Cohn, Kenneth H., and Douglas E. Hough, eds. *The Business of Healthcare, Volume 1—Practice Management*. Westport, CT: Praeger, 2007, pp. 93–106.

YOUR PRACTICE IDENTITY

As a solo practitioner, *you* are the practice identity. Usually, patients come to see you because they were referred by a friend or a physician. Patients will usually stay in your primary care practice if they like you—unless they are driven off by other factors. Primary care physicians will generally continue to refer patients to those of you who are specialists if they (and their patients) like you. In group practice settings, new patients are most frequently referred to a specific primary care physician, by name, rather than to the group or location. In fact, one of the major complaints heard in busy group practices is patients not being able to see "their own" doctor—another indicator of the patient's preference for a personal relationship with a physician. The name and reputation of a practice are certainly critical in competitive markets, but we say again, *you* are the practice identity for most new patients. Consequently, when promoting your practice, *you* should be the primary focus, and your group affiliation(s) should take a secondary position.

DIRECT-TO-CONSUMER PROMOTIONAL TACTICS

Those who we see as patients usually see themselves as customers. (If we see children, their parents are our customers.) It is a well-documented fact that women are the health care purchasers for the family.[2] Therefore, women are the primary customer for those specialties to whom patients commonly self-refer. It is also well understood that primary care practices grow largely through word-of-mouth referrals from other satisfied patients. The key to success for new practices is *establishing* the referral momentum in the first place. The key to success for established practices is *maintaining* an appropriate referral momentum without overwhelming the physician or the staff—especially as the practice reaches maturity.

Today, consumers are inundated with promotional messages. Think of the number of messages vying for your attention each day: television ads, radio spots, billboards, Internet pop-ups, e-mail spam, newspaper ads, magazine ads, direct-mail fliers, telemarketers, salespeople, and others. Most of us cannot process what we already encounter on a daily basis, so we ignore most of it as background noise. In such an environment, the most effective way to deliver your message to the ultimate consumer is through your own passive sales force—namely, your established patients.[3] Word of mouth is, by far, the best way to "grow" a primary care practice. Your sales force will circumvent all the promotional noise clamoring for the attention of your potential patients. Someone asks for advice on the selection of a physician, and they receive an opinion from a trusted friend or relative. That opinion becomes a testimonial of sorts, usually directed toward the friend's own doctor. For this reason, your commitment to "customer" service and your insistence on the same from your support staff is your primary promotional tool (and a reflection of your identity). In fact, all other promotional efforts will be wasted if your new customers do not have a positive experience when they actually contact and visit your practice.

Still, a new practice must have more than word of mouth to develop that initial bolus of patients who will begin to "sell" your practice to their friends and relatives. There are several proven methods to introduce your practice to the community. For specialties

---

[2]Braus, Patricia. *Marketing Health Care to Women: Meeting New Demands for Products and Services.* Ithaca, NY: American Demographics Books, 1997, p. 2.

[3]Halley, Marc. *The Primary Care–Market Share Connection: How Hospitals Achieve Competitive Advantage.* Chicago, IL: Health Administration Press, 2007, p. 38.

needing to promote directly to the consumer, newspaper advertising is a great way to reach a lot of people right out of the chute. Granted, a newspaper ad is a shotgun approach. Many of those who receive your message will not even pay attention to it, because they live too far away from your practice (most primary care relationships are developed close to home), they already have a satisfactory relationship with a physician, or they are not motivated to consider medical care at the moment. Nevertheless, some will respond to a well-written advertisement and will give your practice a call. A newspaper ad is a relatively inexpensive way to reach a lot of people quickly. We recommend running the ad multiple times during the first few months. We also recommend that the ad include a nice professional picture of you; your name, address, and phone number; your specialty and credentials; and most importantly, your major areas of clinical interest shared in layman's terms (e.g., special interest in headaches or women's health). Your selected newspaper will likely be able to tell you how to best reach your consumer audience given their readership, and you can compare the costs and benefits of this investment. The newspaper can also usually help you with the design of an advertisement, as can most local hospital marketing departments.

After a relatively short period of time, usually less than sixty days, we typically recommend shifting your promotional focus to direct mail (if it is available in your community). A professional 8 × 10 sheet that mirrors your newspaper ad (with a picture and so on) can often be delivered to specific homes in neighborhoods within a five- to seven-mile radius of your practice location (you may need a much broader distribution in a rural setting). Direct-mail deliveries can be made quarterly for the first year, depending on your budget and the response you get after each mailing, so track how people find out about your practice as a routine part of new patient information. We have worked with companies in some larger communities that will help to identify the households in your targeted geographic area and then deliver your direct-mail piece to each home (e.g., http://www.flierforhire.com).

As mentioned earlier, more than any other factor, *you* are the identity of your practice—even in a group setting. Getting out and about should be another critical part of your promotional efforts. In most cases, a physician's personal presence is the most powerful sales tool. The following are a few ideas for you to consider:

- **Live in the Community You Serve:** Where you live delivers a powerful message about your commitment to the community. This statement is particularly critical in smaller communities, but it counts in larger suburban areas as well.
- **Be an Active Member of the Medical Staff:** Be active as a member of the medical staff of your selected hospital. If you are a primary care physician, your service will set you apart, because many primary care physicians use the hospitalists and don't darken the hospital doors very often. If you are a specialist, help to protect the interests of your referring physicians by actively participating in medical staff decisions.
- **Meet the Hospital Nurses:** In our experience, the hospital nursing staff is often questioned about physician competence and behavior.
- **Meet Local Pharmacists:** Local pharmacists are often a source of new patients for primary care offices. Meet the pharmacists who your patients are likely to use in your geographic area. Treat them as important partners, and they will become important partners.
- **Attend Church:** If you choose to participate with a local religious congregation, you will find multiple opportunities to be of service, and some of your fellow parishioners will feel comfortable selecting you as their personal physician or recommending you to others.

- **Be a Team Physician:** Depending on your community, football, basketball, or other high school sports can be a major draw for community members. If you have an interest, becoming a team physician can increase your visibility in the community as you walk along the sidelines or out on the floor during games.

- **Speak Often . . . And More Often:** In our experience, having a physician share his or her knowledge, even for only fifteen minutes, always produces new patients. Have your office manager contact day care centers, nursing homes, women's social groups, and other similar organizations to see if they would be interested in a fifteen- or thirty-minute speech from you on a popular health care topic. We have seen family medicine and pediatric physicians approach local elementary schools for opportunities to speak, with immediate results (new patients within the week). Your local hospital probably has a speaker's bureau in which you can also participate. Your state medical association or civic groups may also have speaking opportunities in your target market area.

- **Yellow and White Pages:** It is critical that patients who are trying to find you can do so by looking in standard directories found in your community. In our experience, the vast majority of new patients are referred to your practice through word of mouth, but the second most often quoted source (usually less than twenty percent) is a telephone directory. Make sure you are in the directory both alphabetically and by specialty. A large display advertisement is very expensive and usually not necessary in most communities. (If this tactic is used by your key competitors, however, you may need to be equally visible.)

- **Signage:** Appropriate external and internal (if in a multiuse or multiprovider building) signage is an important means of advertising your practice for those who are trying to find you. There may be significant zoning or landlord restrictions on signage, so be sure to check those out before spending any money on the creative and technical (e.g., size and lighting) requirements of your sign. Within those limits, design a sign that, at a minimum, displays your name, your specialty, and your logo (if applicable). "Accepting new patients" is an important message that may catch the attention of prospective patients whether it is part of the permanent sign or only a temporary banner periodically used to help highlight your availability for patients who can self-refer.

There are many ways to become and remain visible in your community. Taking advantage of those opportunities will help you to establish a busy practice in the shortest amount of time.

A basic practice brochure is an important marketing tool that you will want to include in your initial set of promotional materials. You can carry your brochure and business cards with you to community speaking events, health fairs, and other activities. A brochure is also an important educational tool for patients who select your practice; it contributes to proper management of their expectations. Typically, a brochure will include:

- A professional photo of each provider
- Your logo (if you have one)
- Information about the best way to reach the practice during and after hours for appointments, prescription refills, and test results
- A simple map to reach your location from major thoroughfares
- Perhaps your vision statement for the practice
- The basic services you make available
- The hours you are open for appointments each week

- Perhaps some general information about you and your professional interests
- A discussion of financial matters
- Any unique characteristics of the practice that you wish to highlight

Usually, practice brochures are relatively simple documents, with four to six panels available to display your information, so you will need to be concise. With the availability of software, a designer can lay out the text for a few hundred dollars so that printers can quote their fees for producing the document.

REFERRAL SOURCE PROMOTIONAL TACTICS

Physician specialists who are dependent on others for some or all of their patients/cases face a different promotional challenge than primary care physicians, whose patients can self-refer. Most people, even educated people, and even with the help of the Internet, still don't understand what an otorhynolaryngologist does and when they need to see one. Nor do they have the experience to know when an oncology, rheumatology, or general surgery referral is indicated. In fact, to most people, "the doctor" is a primary care provider, who becomes a trusted friend and advisor. Most patients are totally dependent on their primary care physician for referrals to other specialties.[4]

Specialty physicians have at least two customer segments they must properly address to build and maintain a successful practice. First, they must acknowledge the referring physician or other provider (e.g., nurse practitioners or physician assistants) as a critical "customer." Second, and equally important, they must treat the referred patient as a customer if they expect to receive additional referrals from that referring physician.[5]

Promoting your practice to referring physicians is based on two important tenets[6]:

"Referrals follow relationships."
and
"All relationships atrophy over time."

This means that new specialty practice promotion must include three critical steps. First, new physicians must alert potential referring physicians to their services (particularly unique services or expertise) and availability. Second, new physicians must build personal relationships with potential referring physicians. Third, new physicians must deliver outstanding performance to referring physicians and to their patients.

Alerting new physicians to your services and availability commonly involves the following tactics:

- **Mass Media Advertising:** Although not likely to impact potential patients, a brief newspaper announcement can alert other members of the medical staff to your arrival. We do not recommend more than one or two ads over the first few weeks.
- **Formal Notice:** A nice formal announcement (e.g., wedding announcement quality), hand-addressed to individual physicians, will often make it to the doctor's desk. The formal notice should include information about your training, your practice location, and your areas of clinical interest, and it may also include a Rolodex or business card for future reference.

---

[4]Ibid., p. 35.

[5]Ibid., p. 11.

[6]Ibid., pp. 120–121.

- **Medical Staff Announcements:** Many hospitals have a variety of devices used to communicate with members of their medical staffs. Periodic newsletters, bulletin boards, mailers, and other tools might be used to announce your presence for little or no cost.

Building relationships involves your time, and while your practice is new, you will likely have some excess time. Take advantage of this extra time to get out and visit potential referring physicians. Hospitals will often have liaisons who can arrange such visits, but if not, have your office manager contact their offices and arrange a time for you to make brief visits, either during lunch or before or after office hours. Yes, you can meet some physicians in the medical staff lounge, but we recommend visiting their home turf. You might consider taking a business card, an office brochure, or specialty clinical information that might be unique to your practice. If you are using a special physician referral telephone line in your office (which we recommend), you might share that number with the potential referring physician. If your visit goes well, you might discuss common issues found on your referring physician profile, such as how and when the primary care physician prefers to receive feedback on patients he or she has sent to you for evaluation. Once you have completed this initial visit, it is wise to follow up with a personal letter thanking the physician for his or her time, restating what you learned, and reiterating your availability. As you begin seeing patients who have been referred to you by another provider, always send a follow-up letter to the provider after the patient visit that describes the diagnosis and recommended treatment plan (when appropriate) and thanks this physician for the referral.

Delivering outstanding performance to referring physicians and their patients will also build your relationship with physicians who decide to try "the new person in town." Make sure that your hours, your policies, your procedures, and your staff training are all geared toward ensuring an excellent experience for your customers. Meeting their expectations will do more to promote your practice than any other tactic. We will discuss the concept of customer service in the next section.

CUSTOMER SERVICE AS PRACTICE PROMOTION

Patients are customers. The mothers of your "little patients" are customers. Referring physicians and other providers are customers. Anyone who is a patient, who cares for a patient, or who refers a patient is, by definition, a customer or potential customer of your medical practice.

Customers have certain needs and expectations about their interaction with you and your office staff. If you meet or exceed those needs and expectations, your customer will be pleased. Importantly, your customers will also likely share their positive experience with others, including their referring physician, who can send other customers in your direction. If your customers are disappointed with you, your team, or their experience in your office, they will also likely share their experience with others, including their referring physician. Providing excellent customer service to patients, to their parents and caregivers, and to referring providers is, therefore, essential to your success. In fact, of all the practice promotional tools available, a positive reputation is the most valuable.

When a practice is small and you have a lot of time to spend with patients, you can ensure quality customer service just by your presence. You can easily be responsive to referring physicians. As your practice develops and becomes increasingly busy, however, the time available to spend with patients and to respond to referring physician inquiries is diminished. Busy practices that remain successful depend on developing a culture that "automates" excellent customer service. It becomes second nature—"the way we do things around here." How does one develop that customer-oriented culture? The following suggestions may help:

- **You:** As mentioned earlier, *you* are the identity for your practice. Likewise, *you* are the driver of a customer service culture. Your stated philosophy, your comments on busy days, your attitude toward difficult patients and demanding referring physicians, and most importantly, your actions will set the service standard for your medical practice. If you "pitch a fit" every time your staff tries to work a patient into your schedule, you clarify your real attitude toward your customers—and your staff will reflect that attitude.

- **Your Staff:** The people you hire represent you to your customers. They represent you with patients, their caregivers, and their referring physician. They represent you on the telephone, at the front desk, in the examination room, and at the cashier's window. Hiring friendly, outgoing, and caring people is critical to your success in building a customer service culture. Making sure that they have the training, tools, and time to fulfill their assignments is also essential to their/your success. For example, do not give your receptionist so many assignments that he or she cannot properly greet patients when they arrive and monitor them in the reception area once they are seated.

- **Your Office Policies and Procedures:** Make sure that every office policy, every operating procedure, every patient form, and even your invoices are friendly and professional. Never approve or implement a policy, procedure, or form that does not maintain or enhance customer service—even if it makes your world more efficient! (Granted, there may be some legal/regulatory requirements that must be implemented regardless of their impact on customer service.)

- **Setting:** Make sure your practice setting is warm and inviting without being extravagant. Avoid "bulletproof glass" at the reception window. Glass does not promote the kind of friendly atmosphere required in customer-oriented office. Some will say that glass is required to meet regulations. Boloney! Just be quiet behind the front desk. Make sure everything has a place, and is kept in its place, to reduce any appearance of chaos. Make sure the reception room is neat, clean, and properly furnished.

- **Measure:** Experienced managers know that anything we measure improves. Measuring customer service can be as simple as a quick questionnaire offered to patients as they leave your practice. It can be as easy as asking a referring physician if you and your staff are meeting his or her needs, as a professional. Keep track of the responses. Discuss them in your staff meetings, and set goals to improve your performance as a team.

PROMOTING YOUR PRACTICE FOR LIFE

Practice promotion is not an event or a short-term process. Properly viewed, it is a career commitment for you and for your staff members.

The busier your practice becomes, the more vulnerable you become to patients experiencing frustration, which they share with others, including the referring physician. The busier your practice becomes, the easier it is for a wise competitor to offer improved access and levels of service to your referring physicians. Even if you maintain a great customer service culture, changes in the payer or competitive environment may "rock your world."

The local hospital may employ a specialty competitor and instruct their employed primary care physicians to support the employed specialist. A competing hospital or medical group may purchase primary care practices and employ physicians who have been loyal to you and your hospital. Payers may put additional downward pressure on reimbursement, making it difficult for you to negotiate fair rates of pay for your services. Regardless of the challenge—and there will be many over the years—having a constant flow of new patients will help you to weather the storm.

For primary care providers and specialty physicians, Halley Consulting has developed a "Retail Readiness Questionnaire" that you should review with your staff members on a quarterly basis (contact us at http://www.halleyconsulting.com). Keep track of your score, and select a few new tactics each quarter to improve that score. Discuss your tactics and your performance progress in monthly staff meetings, at a minimum.

Also for specialty physicians, Halley Consulting has developed a "Specialist of Choice Questionnaire" that you should review with your support staff members on a quarterly basis. Keep track of your score, and set a few new performance improvement objectives each quarter. Then, monitor your progress in monthly staff meetings.

Remember, as the physician, *you* are the practice identity. Your name and reputation are on display every time the phone rings or the door opens. Paying attention to the needs, wants, and priorities of your customers—and doing your best to meet those needs, wants, and priorities—will guarantee that you will be successful at attracting new customers, be they patients or referring physicians.

Practice promotion does not require a huge budget or a full-time marketing staff. It doesn't even require a website. What it does require is making sure that the right people are aware of your availability, that you are accessible, and that you meet customer expectations when they do give you a try. Continuously paying attention to the message you are sending as you treat every patient and respond to every referring physician extends your initial promotional momentum for the life of your practice.

CHAPTER Eight

PREPARING FOR OPERATIONS

Your experience and training, as well as the clinical needs of your patients, will largely define *what* services you provide in your medical practice. The wants and priorities of your customers (both patients and referring physicians) will likely define *when* and *where* you provide your services. *How* you will provide your high-quality clinical care will largely be defined by you (the physician) as reflected in the systems, processes, policies, methods, and business procedures that you establish in your medical practice. Practice operations management is the process of defining *how* you will combine your facilities and equipment with your human resources to meet, effectively and efficiently, the needs, wants, and priorities of your patients, of referring physicians and other customers. *Effectively* means getting the job done. *Efficiently* means doing the job in a way that meets the customers' demands while being profitable to you so that you can continue practicing.

This chapter highlights some of the key operational systems, policies, and methods that you will want to define to achieve operational effectiveness and efficiency.

FURNISHINGS AND EQUIPMENT

Furnishing and equipping the physical office site will require the same careful planning and time commitment you have dedicated to previous topics. The acquisition and placement of furnishings and equipment will affect the comfort of your patients as well as your staff (many of whom will spend 40 or more hours a week sitting in that office chair you are about to purchase). During your facility selection, you will have considered the size of the space, the number of exam rooms needed, and the storage and office space in a general sense. Now you must consider how each space will be used so you can furnish and equip each room properly.

We recommend starting the process with several simple copies of your space plan or layout, ideally set to scale. Using a red pencil, trace the traffic patterns that patients will take as they visit your office, being particularly sensitive to the physical locations where the patients will wait. Consider the patient entering and being welcomed to your facility, waiting in your reception area, moving to an examination room, receiving ancillary services, seeing your cashier and appointment desk, and departing. Consider the number of patients likely to be in your facility at any given time, including times when you might be running behind schedule. What furnishings will be needed to accommodate your patients and their chaperones in reception, in the examination room, at the draw station, and so on?

Ideally, this thought process is a repeat of your space planning experience (if you designed your own office). If not, this exercise is very critical, especially now.

Next, take a blue pencil, and identify how you and your staff members are likely to move throughout the day as you fulfill your responsibilities. Where will you and your team most likely need workspace, storage space, space for clinical equipment, and space for business equipment? Some of the shortcomings of existing space can be overcome by selection and proper placement of furnishings and equipment. For example, file cabinets can be used as sound barriers or to enhance privacy in some settings. An extra fax machine in the back office can be an inexpensive way to reduce traffic from the back office to the front office and can keep nursing staff near their assigned locations to enhance physician productivity (just make sure to plan for an extra phone jack for that fax machine).

Finally, compile your furniture and equipment lists for each room into a summary format, and approach several vendors for bids. Let them know that you are bidding out your start-up equipment needs. Review those bids carefully to make certain you understand your financing options and costs, maintenance plan costs, and associated expendable supply costs (particularly on major clinical or business equipment). The initial machine costs may appear to be reasonable, but beware of the hidden operating costs, such as very expensive ink cartridges or reagents. Also remember that any specialty furniture and large equipment will likely take six to eight weeks for delivery, so make certain you allow for this window of time plus the needed setup time. Check with the vendors about the delivery options as well. You may be able to negotiate the actual equipment setup as part of the acquisition. Importantly, once all bids and pricing have been accumulated, you will want to compare them with your capital budget to make sure you have sufficient funds for these purchases. If not, some careful paring of the list may be required.

DETERMINE PRACTICE DOCUMENTATION NEEDS

Believe it or not, the forms and other printed materials you use in your practice will impact your productivity and that of your staff, your service to your customers, and even your financial viability. When you purchased your practice management system, you likely discussed several types of forms required by or produced by the system. There will, however, be other forms as well. Consider forms in the following categories:

- Patient registration
- Patient medical charts
- Patient billing
- Compliance forms
  - Occupational Safety and Health Administration (OSHA)
  - Clinical Laboratory Improvements Act (CLIA)
  - Health Insurance Portability and Accountability Act (HIPAA)
- Authorizations
- Patient education materials
- Clinical support documents
- Marketing materials

Perhaps the most critical form, from a business perspective, is the charge ticket, or "superbill." The charge ticket is usually generated by the practice management system and accompanies the patient throughout the visit. The form facilitates documentation of the services actually provided during each visit and initiates the revenue capture cycle, including point-of-service collections. Regardless of your practice specialty, the super-bill will need to include several key components. A composite list of the most frequently utilized Current Procedural Terminology (CPT) codes and the most commonly encountered diagnosis codes will enable both quick and accurate coding as well as data entry. (Include some additional lines for physicians to write in uncommon procedures or diagnosis codes.) The form will likely have an area for pertinent patient demographic data, which is verified by the receptionist each time the patient visits the practice. Billing or revenue cycle information, including billing and balance forward data, as well as space for recording the method and amount of point-of-service payments will also be included on a well-designed charge ticket. In addition, it is helpful to include return appointment indicators to alert the cashier about the need to schedule any follow-up appointments. Charge tickets are usually numbered sequentially to ensure that missing tickets are found, that clinical documentation occurs, and that charges are properly entered. It is imperative that all super bills are accounted for each day to ensure that the practice captures all revenue.

Some practices use a two-part form for the superbill so that a copy remains with the chart. The patient is asked to take the top copy to the cashier, who will facilitate the checkout process. This approach facilitates documentation, allows the cashier to collect appropriate fees and schedule follow-up visits, and provides backup documentation if the fee ticket walks out the door with the patient.

Similar to the charge ticket, you should consider the use of each form required for the practice and then design each form to most efficiently and effectively meet its designated purpose. It is often helpful to start with copies of forms being used by other practices in your same specialty and, as you discover your own preferences, modify those designs over time.

The following table lists many of the forms to consider in setting up your medical practice. This is not a complete list, but it should provide you with a place to begin. You will also need to verify any local and state regulatory requirements affecting your forms or their design. In addition, you should consult your individual specialty board to obtain guidelines for "best practice" documentation standards of your specialty.

As in all areas, the government has established safety and billing regulations that affect the selection and design of some forms required within your practice. Consider the safety regulations that will govern your practice in the area of clinical processes, such as laboratory testing, invasive procedures, injections, phlebotomy, disease exposure, and hazardous materials exposure. Also consider billing requirements for government and private insurance carriers. Some helpful websites include:

- http://www.osha.gov to learn more about the Occupational Safety Hazards Act and its required protocols and reporting.
- http://www.fda.gov/cdrh/clia to learn more about CLIA and the standards associated with your practice. You may need to search your local state government website as well.
- http://www.hhs.gov/ocr/hipaa/ to learn more about HIPAA.
- http://www.cms.hhs.gov to review Medicare and Medicaid billing policies.
- Visit your state department of insurance website for local regulations.
- Your local medical society or the local Medical Group Management Association may also be a good resource.

Title	Description	Regulatory Implications	Best Practice
Patient registration forms			
New Patient Registration Form	Used to collect all the pertinent demographic and insurance data. Usually contains an authorization to treat and an assignment of benefits clause.	X	X
Established Patient Registration Form	Typically produced by your billing software to facilitate verification that information has not changed.		X
Notice of Patient Privacy Act	Used to identify the laws and regulations regarding patient privacy in regards to protected health information.	X	X
Acknowledgement of Receipt of Patient Privacy Notice	Document retained by the clinic to indicate the privacy notice was received by the patient.	X	X
Patient Arrival Log	This sign-in log indicates the time the patient arrives, the appointment time, the patient name, and the physician to be seen. New privacy rules govern the types of forms that can be used to gather these data, which are helpful in tracking patient flow times.	X	X
Request for Medical Records	Used when patients request their medical records to be shared with another provider or other entity. This request must contain certain legal language, and the release of records must follow a certain protocol.	X	
Telephone Message Form	Used to identify the caller's name and the nature of the call. Often retained in the patient's record to document communication and resolution.		X
Charge ticket, Superbill, Fee Slip	Typically generated by the practice management system for each visit. Contains necessary information to accurately record, code, and bill for services rendered.	X	X
Appointment Reminder Cards	Used to assist patients to remember upcoming appointments.		X
Medical chart forms			
Past Medical and Social History	Typically a questionnaire completed by the patient before medical services that indicates the patient's medical history	X	X
Progress Note	Physician's documentation of the patient encounter. Some physicians use detailed templates. Others prefer a detailed SOAP note. Regardless of your preference, the more detailed the service description, the easier it is to defend your choice of billing codes.	X	X
Continuing Medications List	Ongoing list of medications currently prescribed. Indicates the initial date of prescription and any changes in dosage or discontinuance.		X

Title	Description	Regulatory Implications	Best Practice
Medical chart forms *Continued*			
Problem Summary List	Gathers chronic problems in one location in the chart for easy review.		X
Consent to Treatment Forms	To be signed by patients before procedures or specific treatments to indicate that the risks have been explained. These forms will vary depending on medical specialty and the nature of the procedure.		X
Patient Education Materials	Available from a multitude of resources to provide explanations of prescribed treatments, disease processes, and so on. Each office should maintain an archive of this clinical information in either electronic media or hard-copy form.		X
Specific Health Tracking forms (e.g., immunization, growth, glucose)	These forms will be specific to the medical specialty and can most often be found on state health department websites or obtained through pharmaceutical representatives and medical supply vendors.	X	X
Laboratory forms			
Laboratory Order Requests	These forms are often provided by the outside laboratory services vendor. If laboratory services are provided by the practice, an order form should be developed to ensure order accuracy.		X
CLIA Controls	Depending on the types of laboratory services performed, certain recurring control tests will need to be completed and recorded.	X	X
Refrigerator/Freezer Temperature Logs	Required to ensure the refrigeration units are operating properly and to avoid potential sample contamination.	X	
Sanitation logs	Used to document that the laboratory area has been properly sanitized to avoid test contamination or hazardous exposure.		X
Autoclave Log	Used to document that proper equipment maintenance and sterilization procedures have been followed.		X
OSHA forms			
Tuberculosis skin test acknowledgements and results (employees)	No longer a federal requirement but still strongly recommended. Any staff with potential exposure to patients who have tuberculosis should be tested.		X
Medical Safety Data Sheet listings	Used to identify any hazardous material found in the practice and the specifics regarding the handling and exposure risks of each item. These forms can be obtained from outside vendors.	X	X

Continued

Title	Description	Regulatory Implications	Best Practice
OSHA forms *Continued*			
OSHA Form 300	Provided on the OSHA website (http://www.osha.gov). The required reporting tool when a patient or employee has been injured or exposed to a dangerous substance.	X	X
Patient billing forms			
Payment Arrangement Form	Used to identify acceptable payment terms for payment on account. Typically signed by the patient.		X
Patient Statements	Typically generated by the practice management system or an outside statement processor.		X
CMS 1500 (formerly known as the HCFA 1500 before the Health Care Financing Administration became the Centers for Medicare and Medicaid Services)	The required billing format for reimbursement by insurance carriers, although claims should be filed electronically whenever possible.	X	X
Advanced Beneficiary Notice	Provided by Medicare, and should be given to any Medicare patient receiving medical services that may not/will not be covered.	X	X
Daily Batch Sheet	Used to summarize daily transactions for reconciliation purposes.	X	

DETERMINE MEDICAL SUPPLY NEEDS

Next to labor and building occupancy costs, medical supplies usually account for the next highest expenditure in many medical practices. Some medical supply costs are obvious, such as the costs of the supply itself and of shipping to your location. Other costs are less obvious, however, and usually involve the inventory of supplies that must be stored, counted, transferred, insured, and even disposed of when their shelf life has expired. For example, the "great deal" you got on a million tongue depressors is not such a deal if you only use 400 a month! You and your team will be tripping over tongue depressors for the next several years. Your inventory of supplies should "turn over" as often as reasonably possible given the available storage space and the ability of vendors to respond. Many practices carry no more than sixty or ninety days of inventory—and even less for items that are readily available at a reasonable price. Most vendors will deliver supplies on a weekly basis and will respond to urgent needs immediately, so there is no need to carry a large inventory of most supplies.

The medical supplies category normally includes small items, such as alcohol or cotton swabs, perhaps casting supplies or splints, and pharmaceuticals. You will need to consider additional items that are specific to your specialty, your style of medical practice, and the services you contemplate providing in your practice. Most medical supply vendors can also provide a list of supplies for you to consider (or at least a list of supplies that they provide). Again, considering the activities for each room in your office is a good method for determining which supplies will be needed. Considering the number of patients you are likely to see during the first three months, according to your initial projections, is also a good way to determine you initial inventory needs. We recommend that you complete your full list of medical supply needs and then work with multiple vendors to obtain the best overall pricing in each major category (e.g., pharmaceuticals, orthopedic supplies, and surgical supplies). Another important point to consider when working with your medical supply vendor is to ask for start-up package deals. Given a large initial order, you may be able to negotiate a bulk order discount. Also, look for opportunities to participate in purchasing groups affiliated with your local medical society or local hospital. These purchasing groups may have established pricing discounts with certain medical supply vendors in your area. (At the same time, do not just assume that the group gets the best deal.)

Pharmaceutical supply representatives can also be a great resource to you and to your patients. They typically will provide samples of their preferred medications and some basic medical and office supplies. Check with the representatives regarding other products they may be able to offer, such as patient education materials. You can talk with other local physicians in your specialty to identify local pharmacy representatives, but the representatives will likely find you first.

In terms of maintaining inventory for immunizations, you will want to be extremely cautious. Several vaccines require specific temperatures for proper storage. Others have relatively short shelf lives and must be disposed of if they exceed those limits. Vendors rarely give credit for expired medications, so maintaining enough doses to cover your needs without waste is extremely important. Before the practice stocks a new vaccine, you should verify that it will be covered by the majority of your patients' insurance carriers. If not, you could end up providing the doses "free" of charge to your patients depending on the contracts you have in place.

We also recommend that you check with your local Medicaid provider for access to programs that offer free or low-cost vaccines to children. Most states have made child wellness and vaccination programs a top priority and may offer to supply some vaccines at no cost to you or the patient. These are great programs to ensure child welfare and defer the costs of providing immunizations to those patients who are enrolled. Be aware, however, that these vaccines can only be administered to children who are enrolled in the vaccine programs.

One often-overlooked item in your initial inventory is a mercury spill kit. If you will be using blood pressure cuffs, thermometers, or any other device containing mercury, it is a safety regulation to have a mercury spill kit on hand at all times.

DETERMINE PERIODICALS AND SUBSCRIPTIONS NEEDED

Published resources for continuing medical education, those covering relevant practice management topics, and those needed for clinical or business reference are critical to your success. As you know, a variety of journals, newsletters, and other publications are clamoring for your attention. Most of these periodicals contain potentially useful information. Some (usually the most expensive) present their content in a concise format; others are less efficient reads. You will likely have some preferred journals that you frequently review and reference publications that you want or need to have at your disposal. As your practice becomes busier, your time to review journals and access publications will be at a premium, so consider the most efficient reading route. Keep in mind that accumulating mountains of magazines and shelves of books is no longer a necessity. Look for electronic versions available online or perhaps copies of CD-ROM versions. Electronic media often allow you to search for particular information more quickly and to eliminate office clutter as well.

Check with your local medical societies or the hospital medical staff office, because they will often offer access to certain publications at little or no cost to you.

In addition to clinical publications, you and your team will need access to certain business reference books. Four of the most commonly identified reference books are:

- *International Statistical Classification of Diseases and Related Health Problems, Ninth Revision* (ICD-9)
- *Current Procedural Terminology* (CPT)
- *Healthcare Common Procedure Coding System* (HCPCS or "Hick-Picks")
- *National Correct Coding Initiative Coding Policy Manual for Medicare Services* (NCCI manual)

These reference materials are available in paper and an electronic format. You will likely only need one copy of the NCCI manual (for your staff involved in billing and coding); you may need multiple copies of the other three reference manuals. Because of the cost of a software license for multiple users, it may be more cost-effective initially to purchase a few hard copies and share them among staff members.

You will also want your practice manager to have access to a useful practice management journal or two. These and other resources (e.g., Medical Group Management Association) can provide training to enhance the skills of your manager as well as a peer group to discuss best practices. Most states have local Medical Group Management Association groups that meet often during the year in addition to periodic regional conferences and an annual conference event.

As you are considering periodicals, do not forget to provide popular reading materials for your patients and their chaperones. Keep these books and periodicals updated, and remove those that look overused or damaged. Weekly periodicals, such as *Newsweek, Time, People*, or *Sports Illustrated*, facilitate this turnover as long as your front office staff remembers to remove older issues. You might also consider contacting one of the subscription services, such as EBSCO Information Services (http://corporate.ebsco.com), and comparing their fees for managing all of your subscriptions.

DETERMINE RADIOLOGY AND LABORATORY SERVICE ARRANGEMENTS

Laboratory Contracting

The patient's insurance carrier will often influence where you send laboratory specimens for analysis. You will potentially need to be familiar with several reference labs, including local and national vendors. Local hospitals may also offer laboratory services. Signing up with one or more of these laboratories is usually painless. Each one will have a specific form with which your office staff will need to become familiar. Some labs will report the results of tests online, and many reference labs will provide a centrifuge and other expendable supplies necessary to prepare the specimen for transfer at no cost to you.

Radiology Services

Viewing radiographs and more complex images is a routine part of most medical practices. You will need to have one or more view boxes and at least one high-speed personal computer with an excellent monitor to review digital films. Previously used view boxes can often be found in local markets, and installing them may be as easy as putting two nails in the wall near a source of electricity. If you prefer flush-mounted boxes, installation is a bit more complex and may require the services of a professional. Make sure that the boxes you purchase have adequate lighting and additional features for your convenience.

With the proliferation of digital radiography, you will want to have a computer that can handle the graphics necessary to efficiently and effectively display the results of magnetic resonance imaging or computed tomography. Your personal computer will need significant RAM (memory) and a graphics card with its own processor. You may want to check with local physicians to see how they are receiving digital images sent from local radiologists. Some patients may come to your practice with a CD instead of traditional films. An appropriately placed, high-quality, flat-screen monitor can improve your efficiency in reviewing images. You may want to consider a private setting, like your personal office, if you will be using the images to discuss radiology results with patients.

Your anticipated patient volume and your specialty may support owning radiology equipment, such as flat-plane x-ray or ultrasound. Offering these ancillary services can be an excellent way to provide supplemental income to the practice and is a great convenience for patients. Some specialties, such as orthopedics or obstetrics, quickly build enough patient volume to make owning the equipment almost mandatory. If your initial volume does not support having an expensive piece of equipment and specialized staff in the office, you may want to consider preparing an x-ray room but not equipping it until your practice grows.

Several alternatives to owning x-ray equipment are adequate for many practices. Although not ideal, you might consider sending the patient to the local hospital. Some medical office buildings have centralized x-ray facilities for use by the professional tenants. Physician or hospital-owned, freestanding imaging centers are also available in some communities.

Time-Sharing Arrangements

In some communities, freestanding diagnostic centers will lease time on high-tech equipment, such as computed tomographic scanners and magnetic resonance imagers. Physicians who routinely refer patients for these services may want to consider the cost/benefit of purchasing a time-share. If properly structured, this equipment time-share will allow you to make a high-quality, convenient service available to your patients. You may also be able to bill both technical and professional components of the service. As always, in these legal/regulatory matters, you should check with a qualified local attorney before proceeding.

POLICY AND PROCEDURE MANUAL

Many small medical practices do not take the time to document key policies and procedures to make them available to support staff members. Of those practices that do take the time to create a policy and procedure manual, many do not maintain that documentation over time.

A policy manual serves several key purposes. First, it defines your expectations as the physician and owner of the practice. Second, a policy manual defines how you intend to comply with important regulatory requirements. Third, a policy manual documents and clarifies how you will employ people. Fourth, a policy manual serves as a training resource for new employees. Of course, none of these purposes can be achieved with an absent or poorly maintained manual.

A well-developed policy manual will usually contain at least the following subsections:

- Employee manual (as discussed in detail in Chapter Six)
- Legal/regulatory compliance plans
- Billing policies and procedures

Compliance Plans

Compliance plans are the documented processes and protocols within a practice to define how physicians and staff will comply with the regulatory requirements issued by the various governing bodies. Your compliance plans should define procedures that will help to ensure accurate claims submission for services performed, proper handling of personal health information, and development of a safe work environment. A compliance plan can reduce the chance of inadvertent error by the untrained employee as well as provide employees with a clear path to report compliance concerns with protection from retaliation.

The two most readily recognized and required compliance plans cover OSHA standards and HIPAA standards. Each of these standards falls under a different arm of the federal government.

The Office of the Inspector General, which is a division of the U.S. Department of Heath and Human Services, manages the HIPAA regulations. The most recognized effect of HIPAA is the privacy laws that govern release of patients' protected health information. Information management, however, is only one component of the regulation. HIPAA also creates a nationwide standard for medical claims submission to payers in an effort to reduce incorrect or fraudulent claims.

It is no secret that creating procedures to follow the new regulations, creating a compliance program, and monitoring performance require resources. In an attempt to assist individual and small group medical practices to understand and comply, the Office of the Inspector General published a compliance program guidance report. This report is found in the *Federal Register*, Volume 65, Number 194. The guidance report assists smaller practices in creating a compliance program. The report contains seven components that regulators believe will provide a solid foundation for an effective program. It also offers a systematic approach to implement the required components of a plan within the limited resources of a smaller organization. The seven compliance plan components are[1]:

1. Conducting internal monitoring and auditing.
2. Implementing compliance and practice standards.
3. Designating a compliance officer or contact.
4. Conducting appropriate training and education.
5. Responding appropriately to detected offenses and developing corrective action.
6. Developing open lines of communication.
7. Enforcing disciplinary standards through well-publicized guidelines.

OSHA and its regulations are focused on safety in the workplace. At a minimum, you will want to document your safety policies in the following areas:

- General office safety
- Hazard communication plan

---

[1]OIG Compliance Program for Individual and Small Group Physician Practices, Office of the Inspector General, U.S. Department of Health and Human Services. As found in the *Federal Register* 65, no. 194 (2000): 59434 (http://www.gpoaccess.gov/fr/retrieve.html; select Volume 65, and enter page number 59434 in the search criteria).

- Exposure control plan
- Hepatitis B disclosure
- Radiation control plan

Within your safety compliance plan, you will designate a safety officer and indicate methods and frequencies for training and education of that person. (Your clinical assistant will likely be an excellent candidate for this role.) Rather than developing a safety plan from scratch, we recommend that you purchase a sample safety compliance plan, which can be edited to fit your organization's needs. Before selecting a sample plan, make sure that it has been approved by OSHA and that it contains all the necessary reporting forms and tools for you to develop the proper protocols within your office.

Billing Policies

Billing policies need to be established before the first patient is seen in the practice. These initial policies will have a lasting effect on your practice's fiscal viability. Several policy manuals are available for purchase through resources such as the Medical Group Management Association bookstore. The future of your practice depends on your ability to collect enough cash each month to pay for all your office expenses and still have enough left over to take home a salary for yourself.

Your policies should set the expectation with your patients that you expect payment for the services you provide to them. Billing policies should also provide you with reasonable assurances that you are capturing every charge possible and are billing in a legal and ethical manner. In addition, the billing policies should define the controls necessary to ensure the honesty and ethics of your employees. This subset of billing policies will touch on items such as cash control, daily reconciliation, receipt generation, and write-offs. Importantly, a policy to define your credit extension terms needs to be in place. This policy will also address the point at which you will terminate care for a patient's failure to meet their financial obligations to your practice. If your patients develop the expectation that they are not responsible for paying you for services, it will be extremely difficult to change that expectation. Finally, be prepared to modify your billing policies as regulations change.

OTHER OPERATING POLICIES

You will start your practice with certain policies in place, but many of your operating policies will likely develop and evolve over time. In actual practice, policies and procedures often derive from efforts to improve performance or to solve problems. As you meet with your staff and identify new ways of doing the work or new "rules" you would like them to follow, instruct your office manager to document these methods and/or rules in a simple electronic format that can be printed for inclusion in your three-ring policy manual. At least annually, review the entire policy manual to make sure that all the policies are still relevant. To keep your manual useable, delete or modify those policies that have become obsolete.

As you develop and evaluate policies over time, remember to subject all operational processes and decisions to four critical filters that drive the success of a medical practice[2]:

---

[2]Cohn, Kenneth, and Douglas Hough, eds. *The Business of Healthcare, Volume 1—Practice Management.* Westport, CT: Praeger Perspectives, 2007, p. 43.

1. Does the decision, policy, or process preserve or enhance clinical quality?
2. Does the decision, policy, or process preserve or enhance service quality?
3. Does the decision, policy, or process preserve or enhance provider productivity?
4. Does the decision, policy, or process preserve or enhance practice financial viability?

If a policy, procedure, method or decision cannot pass all four filters, it should be reworked, modified, or abandoned.

You and your team will likely develop operating policies in at least the following categories:

- Customer service initiatives
- Front office operations, including reception, medical records, appointments, referral management, cashier, and telephone or switchboard
- Clinical operations, including clinical support, chaperones, procedure room, ancillary services, patient results feedback, referring physicians, patient questions, and charting

DISASTER RECOVERY

A disaster recovery plan is not a regulatory requirement, but as many practices have learned during recent years, it is definitely a best practice. Dealing with expected (e.g., hurricanes) or unexpected natural disasters or crimes perpetrated on humanity is an increasingly likely occurrence at some point during your career. Your disaster plan should include consideration for natural disasters common to your geographic area. Weather events or conditions can determine when you decide to close your practice for the safety of your staff and patients. You should have a clear policy advising your staff about dealing with perpetrators (e.g., "give them the money and the drugs without hesitation"). Perhaps it would be unsafe to leave anyone in the building alone after hours in your neighborhood. Make sure your staff knows how to respond to 911 emergencies, be they medical or criminal. Make sure that your electronic data are routinely backed up and taken off-site to a safe location. Consider how you might protect your paper medical records (even making sure they are tightly packed in their shelves each night should a fire occur). At a minimum, your disaster recovery plan should include:

- Emergency plan of action for anticipated events
- Emergency contacts
- Disaster phone tree
- Data recovery process

Having a well-thought-out plan of how to communicate with patients, vendors, and staff during a time of crisis will help your practice to recover from unanticipated events.

CHAPTER Nine

IN BUSINESS

HAVE YOU ARRIVED?

Yes, you have arrived, but only at the starting gate. You have waded through business details and made business decisions based on the best information available, which may not have been much in some cases. Now the fun begins! You get to marry your clinical expertise to the business enterprise you have created. Will all go smoothly? We sincerely doubt it! There are far too many variables in business to ensure a smooth transition from start-up to successful practice, but do not despair. If you have planned well, most of the challenges you will face over the next several days, weeks, and months will be minor issues that can be solved as you work with your office manager, your support staff and your advisors. Take your business challenges in stride, and consider them as opportunities to improve and refine your practice and your team. There are very few emergencies in the business office.

This final chapter provides a few suggestions for managing your going concern. The following sections will review the normal practice development process, how to measure your performance, how to recognize problems, and how to enjoy the fruits of your ultimate success.

STOP, LOOK, AND LISTEN

Stop. Look. Listen. These simple instructions are familiar to most small children learning to cross a street safely, but their application in business is nothing short of profound! One of the common challenges faced by clinicians and successful entrepreneurs alike is to balance the time we spend working *in* the business with the time we should spend working *on* the business. As a clinician, your specialty training and experience will likely make working *in* the business easier and a lot more fun. After all, you became a physician to practice medicine. You are also the chief source of revenue production, which is usually a strong motivator. At the same time, unless the business receives your frequent attention, it will likely fail to achieve its potential and will hamper your freedom to practice as you see fit.

Stop, look, and listen, in our context, simply means that we take time, ideally on a weekly basis, to meet with our manager to look at our performance indicators and to listen to feedback about the performance of the practice. The following paragraphs detail some of the common indicators and feedback that should be part of this routine.

Monitoring the growth of a new practice is a critical part of the start-up process. A "cold start," meaning a practice starting from scratch, will likely take from many months (for a specialty practice) to as much as two years or more (for a primary care practice) to reach financial viability.[1] A new practice may take three to five years to reach its optimum level of performance. The time it takes to grow a practice can be a friend and an enemy. It takes time for a new physician to learn to practice productively, for new staff members to fine-tune their systems and processes as patient and referral volumes increase, to build relationships with referring physicians, and for word-of-mouth referrals to generate enough new business for the practice to become self-sustaining. If used effectively, this time will yield the quality care and caring, the productivity, and the financial viability necessary for long term success. If the practice is not progressing appropriately, however, time becomes an enemy, consuming the financial resources allocated for start-up.

Several key indicators help new physicians, their office managers, and their counselors to monitor the *growth* of the practice. The right indicators will vary by practice specialty, but the following are examples of those common to most practices:

- **Patient Volume:** Monitoring your visit volume and trend provides a primary indicator of practice health. Seeing this volume increase weekly and monthly will be a source of comfort to you and your support staff. Adding support staff as growth stretches your resources will be critical to maintain an appropriate level of customer service. Remember, many specialties have some seasonality to their practice. Primary care providers often see an increase in patient volume during the flu season and a decrease during the hot summer months. These slower months also affect the number of referrals they make to specialists. You might talk with experienced local physicians in your own specialty to see what percentage of annual patient visits they see each month of the year. Over time, you can compare your own experience both within the year and year over year.

- **New Patient Ratio:** The new patient ratio is particularly useful for primary care practices. It is calculated by dividing the number of new patient visits by the number of total patient visits for the reporting period (usually a month). The first few days in practice, your new patient ratio will, of course, be one-hundred percent, but it will quickly drop. Our experience indicates that a healthy cold-start primary care practice will usually be about half-full at the end of the first twelve months and have a new patient ratio between thirty-five and forty-five percent.

- **Referral Tracking:** Procedures and visits produce the revenue, but referrals are the lifeblood of a specialty practice. Smart specialists will want to know all of the potential referring physicians and other providers in their target market area. You will want to meet, network with, and market to these potential referring providers on an ongoing basis (as described in Chapter Seven). Then, you will want to track each physician referral by source, clinical issue, and payer mix each month. Every new referring physician is a positive indicator. Every repeat referring physician is a positive indicator. Physicians who quit referring over time should receive a call to make sure that you have met their needs, wants, and priorities as well as those of their patients.

- **Geographic Mix:** In an urban or suburban setting, primary care practices will likely draw the majority of their patients from a relatively short distance around the medical practice. Most patients will only drive three to five miles to see their

---

[1]Halley, Marc. *The Primary Care–Market Share Connection: How Hospitals Achieve Competitive Advantage*. Chicago, IL: Health Administration Press, 2007.

primary care physician unless they have no other alternative; however, they will drive across town to see a specialist to whom they have been referred by a trusted primary care physician.[2] Tracking the location of new patients is a good indicator of how a primary care practice is growing. Keeping track of new patient zip codes indicates where the practice is growing and can identify neighborhoods that might be vulnerable to new primary care physician competitors. Some new practices place a map of the market area in the break room and put pins in the neighborhoods producing their new patients. (Software is available to accomplish this same purpose.)

- **Payer Mix:** Managing your payer mix is a necessity in a growing practice. The payer mix of new patients should be monitored on a monthly basis by you and your office manager.

Monitoring the growth of your practice is particularly important during the early months, when there is less to do and more time for you and your staff to worry. Having realistic expectations about growth, and frequently monitoring your growth, will help you to "keep the faith" while the practice develops.

On an ongoing basis, you will need to monitor performance in twelve key areas, regardless of your specialty or practice situation. Some years ago, we identified these twelve critical factors that have stood the test of time.[3] The medical practice "game" is won or lost on the revenue side of the income statement. Eight of the twelve critical factors affect practice revenue. The other four factors comprise the key expenses that account for the vast majority of your costs (the expense side), and although these costs can destroy your bottom line and must also be monitored, you will not cost cut your way to financial success in a medical practice. A brief review of the revenue and expense factors is presented next.

Revenue Factors

The eight revenue factors that affect the success of a medical practice are (1) volume/capacity mix, (2) payer mix, (3) fees, (4) customer service, (5) physician productivity, (6) coding and documentation, (7) accounts receivable management, and (8) service mix.

Volume/Capacity Mix

Your medical practice will succeed or fail on volume. Patient visits, patient referrals, work relative value units (WRVUs), consults, laboratory services, radiology procedures, deliveries, and surgeries are all indicators of volume. Capacity is a function of your ability to diagnose and treat patients as well as the ability of your practice (e.g., support staff, systems, and processes) to see that volume of patients efficiently and effectively. Assuming that your selected market has adequate numbers of patients and that you are successful in attracting those patients, either directly or through referrals, your volume will increase markedly over the first two years of practice. Your capacity to deliver your services will increase, as will your confidence, as you become more familiar with the "practice" of medicine and as your medical practice becomes more efficient, based on experience. At some point, however, you will approach your personal capacity. There are only so many hours

---

[2]Ibid.

[3]Halley, Marc D., and Robin L. Lloyd "How to Break Even on an Acquired Primary Care Network." *Healthcare Financial Management* 54, no. 11 (2000): 69–74.

in the day, and you will need rest and recovery time adequate to maintain your health, your family life, and your sanity. In our experience, the most successful medical practices can measure their volume (usually in terms of visits or WRVUs) above the 50th percentile, when compared to others in their specialty. In fact, given reimbursement in most markets, the closer a practice approaches the 75th percentile of performance, the more comfortable the physician is with the medical practice business.

Payer Mix

Payer mix is always a delicate subject. Nevertheless, to avoid bankruptcy, you must watch your payer mix very carefully. New practices often attract those who cannot—or will not— pay for their care. (Some may have been dismissed from other practices for failure to do so.) New practices will also attract those who are uninsured or underinsured. Medicaid patients find it difficult to gain access to care in some communities, because other physicians cannot afford (from a business perspective) to see them (so these patients will seek new providers). Some commercial carriers reimburse at very low levels relative to their competitors, and as a result, their insureds have a difficult time finding access to primary and/or specialty care. If you are a primary care physician, you can easily fill your practice with those who have no other options. Unfortunately, if you lose money on every patient you see, you will not make it up on volume! We encourage our clients to see a fair share of the uninsured and underinsured; however, the reality you face is that you must reserve the majority of your appointment slots for patients who are insured and who do pay for your services. If your market is fortunate enough to have a federally qualified community health center (FQHC) or other similar resource, we encourage you to have that number available for your front desk to share with those who you cannot see. Some of these programs receive significant reimbursement for each visit relative to private practice. (Obviously, if someone presents at your front desk bleeding or with symptoms of a heart attack, stabilize and call 911. Don't worry about their insurance card!) Finally, managing your payer mix may have legal/regulatory implications and payer contact implications for your locale. Please discuss this topic with your local legal counsel.

Fees

Most of the time, your actual reimbursement for the services you provide will be determined through negotiation with local payers or based on prevailing rates, as in the case of Medicare and Medicaid. These rates will likely be well below the actual fees that you and other physicians in your area might charge. Considering this, you might legitimately ask, "So why worry about my fees?" First, your fees should be set above the best-reimbursing payer in your area so that you take full advantage of reimbursement available. (This will mean that you might see heavy discounts, especially for government programs.) Second, setting realistic fees will help you better understand how to manage your payer mix. Third, setting your fees fairly and watching the resulting reimbursement will help you understand how to better manage the services you personally emphasize and the ancillary services you might add to your practice. You should not discuss fees with your competitors. Rather, discuss them with your trusted advisor, and review your fees at least annually, particularly that top twenty percent of your fees that account for eighty percent of your revenues. With a bit of operating history, your actual reimbursement, by payer, will help you to fine-tune your fees.

Customer Service

As a primary care physician, your practice will grow largely by word of mouth, from one patient to another. As a specialist, your practice will grow by word of mouth from one physician to another as patients report back to their referring physician and as you and your staff provide service to your primary care physician customers. Tracking your volume, your new patient ratio, and your referrals, as mentioned above, are effective ways to know if you are delivering as expected. A patient satisfaction survey (and there are many examples on the market) is also a great way to get timely feedback regarding your team and your own performance. Some of the most effective surveys are ten questions or less and ask the respondent about the different areas of your office, from the telephones and appointment desk to your nurse, your care, and the billing office. Importantly, as a specialist, take the time to frequently ask referring physicians if you and your team are meeting their needs. *Take immediate action when you hear complaints or concerns. These events provide opportunities for you to cement relationships by listening and responding to your customers.*

Physician Productivity

Like it or not, your personal productivity will determine the ultimate success or failure of your practice as well as your ability to comfortably pay your home mortgage. In the beginning, you will likely have time on your hands for marketing activities and to help around the office. As your practice becomes busier, you must routinely examine those activities that could—and should—be delegated to others. The more time you spend examining patients, performing procedures, coding and documenting your work, and responding to the needs of your customers, the happier and more successful you will be. If you spend time at your desk doing paperwork that others could do (at a lower rate per hour), you will soon become frustrated. Remember the principles of highest and best use staffing discussed in Chapter Six. Authorize your clinical assistant to manage your productivity by keeping your exam rooms full, keeping your patients comfortable, and keeping you moving. Make sure your assistant is not doing things (like referral calls) that could be moved out of the back office without negatively impacting patient care. Monitor your productivity on a weekly, if not a daily, basis. Track your patient volumes, your total WRVUs, and your WRVUs per patient. You can compare these numbers with your own previous work and with external benchmarks for your specialty.

Coding and Documentation

You have learned to document for clinical purposes. If you are going to be paid fairly, you must also learn to code and document for billing purposes. It is a great idea to have someone with coding experience on your team. It is also great to have a coding module as part of your software package. We always recommend, however, that the physician learn to code and document for billing purposes. You are in the examination room, after all, and you know the services you provided to each patient. Paying a bit of attention to payer requirements can help you maximize your reimbursement for legitimate services you provide. Undercoding is just as serious as overcoding. Always make sure that your services and your documentation of those services are consistent with the code or codes you assign. In the office setting, we recommend coding at the time of service so that the fee ticket can be carried by your patient to the cashier for any point-of-service collections and next-appointment activity. We recommend that you hold a dozen charts for a day or two each quarter and hire a professional coder to examine your coding and documentation in advance of billing the payers. A professional can tell you if you are coding and documenting properly, and you can make any corrections before sending out the bills. This is called a prospective review or audit.

Accounts Receivable Management

The money owed to you by patients and payers for services you have already performed is called accounts receivable. Managing your accounts receivable is critical to ensure the cash flow necessary to make payroll and to pay other bills for the practice. A key indicator of your performance in this area is called "days in accounts receivable," or "days in

A/R." Days in A/R is usually determined by dividing the total amount in your accounts receivable by your average charges per day (charges for the past month divided by 30 days). In most well-managed practices, days in A/R will range between forty and sixty days. This measure indicates how quickly you are collecting your outstanding accounts. Obviously, when you first start your practice, this number will seem to rise quickly, but it will soon level off. If it rises above sixty days, start looking for potential causes, such as a high number of claims rejected or denied by payers or the failure of your cashier to collect patient due balances at the time of service.

Another important indicator of successful accounts receivable management is the age of your receivables. Most billing software and all outside billing vendors should be able to show you the age of your outstanding accounts. Aging is usually divided in thirty-day increments, or "buckets." Ideally, the largest percentage of your total accounts receivable will fall within the thirty- and sixty-day buckets, tapering off rapidly in the buckets for ninety and one-hundred-twenty days. The bucket for more than one-hundred-twenty days might see another small spike or bump representing some patient due balances (if you allow patients to make payments over time), claims your team is still disputing with payers, and slow pays (e.g., some motor vehicle accident claims).

A third important indicator of accounts receivable management is the percentage of your charges that you actually collect (or its reciprocal, the percentage that you write off by contract with insurance carriers). For example, a family physician may charge a patient $100 for services performed. According to the patient's insurance plan, the patient owes you a copayment of $20, which your staff should collect at the time of the office visit. The payer "allows" or approves $50 for the services you rendered, and you have agreed, by contract with the payer, to write off the remaining $30. In this case, your collection rate is seventy percent of your charges, which is indicative of a primary care or cognitive practice. Invasive practices may collect as little as forty percent of charges. You should check your collections percentage (collections ratio) over time and also compare it with published benchmarks for your specialty.

Service Mix

Your service mix involves both *what* services you provide and *how* you provide them. You will likely offer many of the cognitive and invasive services you are trained and qualified to provide. You may choose not to provide some of the services you experienced during your residency program; for example, many family physicians choose not to provide obstetrics even though they had an OB/GYN rotation. Some general internists choose not to provide hospital services even though a portion of their training was specific to inpatient settings. You may also choose to pursue additional training to offer services unique to your practice. For example, some family physicians have chosen to offer endoscopic screening procedures, culposcopy, treadmill stress testing, pulmonary function tests, or bone densitometry testing in their offices. You may choose to make basic laboratory and radiology services available in your office. Many cognitive specialists find that additional procedures and ancillary services are appreciated by patients, increase the physician's enjoyment of practice, and enhance practice income.

How you provide your services is also part of your service mix. Will you offer evening hours or weekend appointments? Will you offer some services in more than one location? Can your patients expect you to follow them if they are admitted to a hospital?

Selecting your service mix should certainly be influenced by your training and comfort level. The "community standard" set by others in your specialty should influence your service mix as well. If patients are used to extended hours in primary care practices, you will need to accommodate that expectation. If primary care physicians are used to same-day response for consults, you will need to meet or exceed that standard. Set your service mix expectations with your support staff so that they understand the evening hours they will need to work or the procedures in which they will be required to assist.

Expense Factors

A number of expenses are associated with operating a medical practice, and the most significant of these costs fall into four categories:

1. The physician is (you are) the most expensive resource, requiring both compensation and personal benefits associated with his or her employment. Physician costs frequently consume between forty and fifty percent of cash in a primary care practice. An invasive specialist, making market-competitive compensation and receiving benefits, may constitute sixty percent or more of the practice cost structure.
2. The cost of employing your support staff, including both compensation and benefits, is the second most significant cost associated with your practice. Depending on the practice specialty and setting, nonphysician labor costs can account for between fifteen and thirty-five percent of medical practice expense.
3. The cost of your physical space (your office lease, utilities, and janitorial expense) can run between four and ten percent of your cost structure.
4. Clinical supplies used to provide services in your office can account for between two and eight percent, again depending on your specialty.

These four expense categories can total eighty-five percent or more of all medical practice expenses. Three of these expenses are largely "fixed" costs in the short term. Whether you see ten or several hundred patients a month, your office rent does not change, for example, and you still pay your clinical assistant and your receptionist. Your clinical supply cost (the only variable cost in the short term) does change as patient volume changes.

Managing your expenses is certainly critical to your success, but as mentioned before, because most of your costs are "fixed" over the short term, the success of your medical practice is dependent on you seeing enough patient volume and generating enough revenue associated with that volume to cover your costs. The "game" is won or lost on the revenue side of the income statement.

PERFORMANCE IMPROVEMENT

During the early days of your practice, when patient volume is still growing, you will have time to think about improving your own skills and the processes or methods you use in your office. You will have more time to stop, look, and listen. As you become increasingly successful, however, this time will disappear, and you will struggle to keep up with the daily demands of the office, the hospital, the nursing home, and so on.

As mentioned earlier, busy physicians and busy practices become vulnerable to inefficiencies that creep into every organization. Processes that worked at lower patient volumes become overwhelmed at higher volumes. Physicians and staff can develop bad habits. Policies, procedures, and job descriptions become outdated. Even the forms we use can become irrelevant over time. Holding a meeting between physicians and management at least once a month to review financial and statistical information as well as practice issues can highlight opportunities for improvement. Making time to have staff meetings can also help identify sources of frustration in daily operations. Occasionally, practices hire outside firms to evaluate practice operations and to identify opportunities for their improvement. Regardless of the source, opportunities to examine and improve your practice will frequently surface.

Methods improvement is a simple approach to tackling these opportunities. In its simplest form, methods improvement involves (1) identifying all of the steps in a process, (2) documenting those steps, and (3) engaging those who do the work in reviewing each step for appropriateness, relevance, redundancy, efficiency, and so on.

Exhibit 9a is a flow chart that identifies the steps of a common process found in most medical offices. Once the steps in the process have been identified, physicians and staff can be engaged in asking critical questions about each step to determine whether it should be removed, modified, or remain unchanged. The following questions might be asked of *each* step:

- What would be the impact of eliminating the step (e.g., cost savings, impact on other steps, impact on clinical quality, service quality, physician productivity, and financial viability)?
- Does the step actually accomplish its purpose?
- In what way does the step add value to the product or service being provided?
- How could inputs (e.g., chart supplies and patient information forms) be improved to streamline or eliminate the step?
- Is there a delay in getting inputs to the step?
- Are all step outputs necessary?
- Can the step be combined with another step and be eliminated as a distinct operation?
- Is the step properly sequenced among all steps in the process?
- Has responsibility for the step been specifically assigned?
- Does the incumbent demonstrate competence in the technical aspects of the step?
- Can the step be assigned to a lower-cost employee?
- Should the step be performed at another time of day?
- Can the step be "batched" (e.g., combined and completed later or outside the real-time process) with improved results?
- Can the step be further standardized?
- Is the step redundant?
- Can the "inspection" be eliminated without materially affecting subsequent steps?
- Can lower-cost materials be used in the step without materially affecting subsequent steps or the output of the process?
- Can materials used in the step be standardized to reduce the number of material types?
- Can the outputs be transported more efficiently?
- Is there delay built into the step? Can it be eliminated?
- How can working conditions be changed to improve the result?
- Can set-up time be reduced or eliminated for the step?
- Are the costs associated with the step worth the benefits?
- How can the step be simplified?
- Would an equipment change improve the step result?
- Should the step be investigated further?

Obviously, even simple methods improvement can consume valuable time and energy. Consequently, it should be used when the problem or opportunity is likely to yield a return

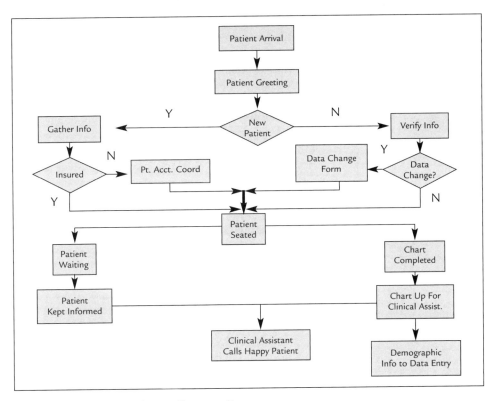

EXHIBIT 9A PATIENT INTAKE PROCESS FLOWCHART

on that time and energy. In addition, busy practices and people can only absorb a limited amount of change at one time. We encourage our clients and their managers to prioritize those performance improvement issues they would like to address over time and then start with those problems that have the greatest potential for return in terms of clinical quality, service quality, provider productivity, and financial viability.

ENJOYING THE FRUITS OF YOUR LABOR

First, enjoy the adventure! You have trained so long and so well. Enjoy providing your clinical services and blessing the lives of those you serve, as well as those you employ. Embrace and learn the business side of your practice as well. It is inextricably tied to your success and enjoyment of the clinical side. Both must receive your attention and energy.

Second, take your own advice! Listen to the counsel you give your patients about taking care of themselves physically and emotionally. Schedule a life outside of your practice without charts to complete or call coverage. Manage your personal energy, and you will be a better physician and business owner. Take time for family, friends, and hobbies. "Doctor" is a wonderful title and comes with well-deserved respect, but it does not define who you are.

Third, surround yourself with great people! Find and pay for an experienced office manager. He or she will be worth every penny in terms of daily operations. Take the time to hire great staff members. They will make or break your practice. Hire a fine accountant, a fine attorney, and a fine financial planner. These trusted counselors can guide your steps and keep you out of trouble in their areas of expertise.

Fourth, avoid unnecessary debt! You probably have debt associated with your training. You will likely have debt associated with your business. You (and perhaps your family) will exit your training program with a lot of pent up demand in the face of income that may be three, four, or more times your residency salary. We have seen so many young physicians succumb to the temptation to buy that huge house or acquire that new car. Remember, the interest on debt never rests. Be conservative in your purchases until your business is on solid footing. Then, you can begin to enjoy the good things of the earth—and there are many! You will also have the ability to start preparing for your retirement rather than just servicing overwhelming debt. (Listen to your financial planner.)

Fifth, share the rewards! Most importantly, share your thanks often with those that help you build a successful practice. Yes, a lot of your success will depend on your ability to perform as you have been trained, but you will not succeed alone. Acknowledge those with whom you journey. As you are able to do so, share some of the financial rewards. We recommend sharing financial rewards in the form of occasional bonuses based on the success of the business.

Congratulations to you for your clinical knowledge and achievements, and welcome to the medical practice business. Like all business ventures, a medical practice is rife with opportunities and challenges, risks and rewards. If you learn and apply correct business principles (many of which are contained in these pages), you will be able to grasp the opportunities, manage the risks and challenges, and reap the rewards of success. Business is like a game. If you learn the rules, you can play well. If not, you will suffer the frustration associated with reduced accomplishment or failure. Learn the rules, and have fun!

accounting
  in business plan of medical practice, 15–17
  objectives supported by, 16
  for solo medical practice, 16
accounts receivable, management system, 15, 59–61,
    119–120
affiliations
  location affecting, 7
  of medical staff of hospitals, 18–19
architects, 29
attorney, real estate, 33

banks
  commercial loans from, 20
  line of credit with, 19
  medical practice's relationship with, 19–20
benefit verification machine, 66
benefits. *See* employment benefits
billing
  forms, 108
  policies, 113
brochures, 98–99
building occupancy, 7
business plans
  accounting in, 15–17
  environmental assessment for, 12
  finance section of, 17–21
  governance in, 13
  human resources in, 14
  legal structure in, 18
  management information system in, 15
  for medical practices, 11–18, 16t–17t
  mission/vision/values in, 12–13
  operations as part of, 14–15
  practice development in, 13–14
  purpose of, 11

business reference books, 110

CAM. *See* common area maintenance
capital
  investment, 17
  operating, 17–18
Centers for Medicare and Medicaid Services (CMS), 38–39
CLIA. *See* Clinical Laboratory Improvement Amendments
Clinical Laboratory Improvement Amendments (CLIA)
  application for certification from, 45
  certification from, 44–45
  levels of certification from, 45
CMS. *See* Centers for Medicare and Medicaid Services
common area maintenance (CAM), fees, 34
communication tools. *See also* telephone system
  for medical practice, 52–54
community, issues and medical practice location, 4–6
competition
  location and, 9
  medical practice location and, 5–6
  saturation/exclusion and, 5–6
compliance plans, 112–113
computers
  hardware, 61
  networks, 61–62
  workstations, 62–63
construction
  changes during, 29
  contractor for, 31
  on office, 28–33
  payments for, 33
  punch list and, 32–33
  remodeling existing space through, 33
  starting, 31–32
  subcontractors for, 32–33
  wires and, 32